DAILY

DEVOTIONAL

FOR WOMEN

Published by Midsummer Bloom Books

First Edition: August 2025
Printed in the United States of America.

CONTENTS

WELCOME, SISTER

Welcome to *Daily Devotional for Women*. I'm so glad you're here. Think of this book as a companion for your everyday life—through busy days, quiet moments, joy, and tears. Let these pages be a gentle reminder: you're seen, you're loved, and you're not walking alone.

Each day, you'll find:

 * A short Scripture (KJV) to anchor your heart.
 * A reflection connecting God's Word to your life—your relationships, work, worries, and dreams.
 * A single question to carry with you.

No long lectures, no heavy theology—just the living Word, brought close to you.

How to Use This Book:

Start wherever you are—January 1st or June 14th, it doesn't matter. Keep it simple. Read the Scripture out loud, let the reflection settle, and sit with the question. Some days may be quick; others may linger. God isn't keeping time—He's keeping you.

Expect God to meet you. He loves to speak to His daughters—through His Word, quiet nudges, and sacred everyday moments.

As you read, may you breathe deeper, feel God's Word near, and remember that Jesus is close—especially to the weary, the wondering, and to you.

Ready? Let's begin, one day at a time.

January: Faith and Trust

Day 1

"Trust in the LORD with all thine heart; and lean not unto thine own understanding." — Proverbs 3:5 (KJV)

Trusting God is a lot like using a GPS you can't always see. You punch in the destination, but the route surprises you—detours, delays, unknown roads. Our understanding wants control, but God sees the long view. He knows what's around the bend and what we can't yet imagine. Trust looks like releasing the white-knuckle grip—on timelines, outcomes, and other people's opinions—and choosing His voice over the loudness of worry. It's pausing before sending the text, breathing before reacting, and asking, "Lord, what's Your way here?" You don't need all the answers to move forward. You need the Answer with you. He's steady, even when the path isn't.

Reflection Question: What would leaning on God—not your own understanding—look like in one decision today?

Day 2

"What time I am afraid, I will trust in thee." — Psalm 56:3 (KJV)

Fear shows up uninvited—during a doctor's call, a late-night worry spiral, or a bill that stretches the budget. David doesn't pretend he's never afraid; he chooses where to place his fear. Trust isn't the absence of shaky knees; it's deciding who holds your hand as they shake. Think of a child reaching for her mother in a crowded store—not because the crowd vanishes, but because presence calms the heart. God's presence does that for you. Whispering, "I trust You," doesn't magically re-move the situation, but it re-centers your soul. It moves the spotlight off the fear and back onto the Father who never leaves.

Reflection Question: When fear rises today, what short prayer of trust will you breathe?

Day 3

"Thou wilt keep him in perfect peace, whose mind is stayed on thee: because he trusteth in thee." — Isaiah 26:3 (KJV)

Perfect peace sounds dreamy, but Isaiah ties it to a very practical habit: where your mind rests. Our thoughts can pace like a worried parent at midnight. Peace comes when we "stay" our minds on God—like setting a screen to "Do Not Disturb." Staying isn't a one-time click; it's a pattern. We return again and again to who God is—faithful, kind, wise, near. As you load the dishwasher or sit in traffic, turn your thoughts toward Him. Peace doesn't mean your life gets quiet; it means your heart learns a new quiet in the noise. Trust anchors your thoughts so they don't drift with every wave.

Reflection Question: What thought will you redirect toward God whenever worry starts today?

Day 4

"Commit thy way unto the LORD; trust also in him; and he shall bring it to pass." — Psalm 37:5 (KJV)

There's relief in handing God the whole map—the route, rest stops, and unknown exits. "Commit" means roll it over onto Him. Not just the big life decisions, but the daily ones too— school choices, work emails, hard conversations, dinner plans when you're exhausted. Trust is the exhale after committing: "Lord, it's Yours." He doesn't need your perfect plan to make good happen. He asks for your surrendered heart. When you commit your way, you invite His timing and His wisdom. He brings to pass what is best—sometimes differently than you imagined, but always better than going it alone.

Reflection Question: What's one plan you can roll onto the Lord and release today?

Day 5

"Blessed is the man that trusteth in the LORD, and whose hope the LORD is." — Jeremiah 17:7 (KJV)

Hope is more than optimism; it's a Person. When our hope hangs on outcomes—promotions, approvals, timelines—it swings wildly with every change. But when the Lord is our hope, blessing roots deep. Like a tree by a river, you draw nourishment from who He is, not from shifting circumstances. Even in drought seasons, trust keeps leaves green. Maybe your calendar is full, but your heart feels empty. Plant your hope by the water of His Word. Blessing isn't always a new thing; often it's a new way of seeing the same thing—with Him in it.

Reflection Question: Where have you hung hope on outcomes, and how can you rehang it on God?

Day 6

"Now faith is the substance of things hoped for, the evidence of things not seen." — Hebrews 11:1 (KJV)

Faith gives shape to the invisible. It's like framing a house before the walls go up—you can walk the outline, even if you can't yet see the paint colors. Faith isn't pretending; it's perceiving. You're trusting God's character before the answer arrives. You hold onto His promises while the hallway still looks dark. That takes courage—and it's okay if it feels wobbly. God isn't grading the steadiness of your step; He's holding your hand. The "evidence" isn't the result; it's the confidence that grows as you keep walking with Him.

Reflection Question: What unseen hope will you frame with faith by trusting God today?

Day 7

"Jesus said unto him, If thou canst believe, all things are possible to him that believeth." — Mark 9:23 (KJV)

This isn't a blank check for our wish list; it's an invitation to trust Jesus with what looks impossible. The mountain may be a strained relationship, a habit you can't shake, or a door that won't budge. Belief shifts your focus from the mountain to the Mountain Mover. He decides the how and when—sometimes He moves it, sometimes He climbs it with you, sometimes He reshapes you through it. Possibility blooms where belief is planted. Bring Him your "I believe—help my unbelief," and watch what His power can do with your honest heart.

Reflection Question: Where do you need to bring your honest belief and unbelief to Jesus today?

Day 8

"Take therefore no thought for the morrow: for the morrow shall take thought for the things of itself. Sufficient unto the day is the evil thereof." — Matthew 6:34 (KJV)

Tomorrow can feel like a crowded inbox—unread and relentless. Jesus invites you to the holy practice of "today." Not careless, but careful in the right way—attentive to the present grace given for this moment. Worry borrows trouble that hasn't arrived; trust receives strength that has. When your mind sprints ahead—to next month's bills or next year's plans—call it back to today's manna. God meets you in daily portions, just enough for now, more than enough because He is with you.

Reflection Question: What is one way you can stay with today's grace instead of tomorrow's worry?

Day 9

"Be still, and know that I am God..." — Psalm 46:10a (KJV)

Stillness can feel impossible when notifications ping and needs pull. But "be still" isn't about perfect quiet; it's about settled knowing. God is God, and you don't have to be. Let that sink in like sun on your face. Put down the imaginary clipboard where you manage everyone's outcomes. Breathe. Whisper His name. The world spins, but He doesn't. When you pause, you make room to recognize His presence in ordinary places—at the kitchen sink, in the car line, on a weary walk. Stillness becomes a doorway to strength.

Reflection Question: Where can you create a small pause today to remember that He is God?

Day 10

"Be careful for nothing; but in every thing by prayer and supplication with thanksgiving let your requests be made known unto God." —
Philippians 4:6 (KJV)

Anxiety loves to make lists. Prayer does too—only it hands the list to God with thanksgiving. Gratitude doesn't deny the need; it acknowledges the Giver. Pour out the specifics: names, numbers, deadlines. Then lace them with thanks for who He is—Provider, Counselor, Father. As you shift from spinning thoughts to spoken prayers, peace starts to guard your heart like a night watch. You don't have to edit yourself with God. He invites the whole story, then offers His steady presence in return.

Reflection Question: What request will you bring to God today—and what thanks will you add?

Day 11

"For we walk by faith, not by sight." — 2 Corinthians 5:7 (KJV)

Walking by sight is simpler—you step where you see. Faith asks you to move when you only have a promise and a Person. It's like driving in fog with low beams; you can't see the whole road, but you can see enough to keep going. God gives light for the next step. Not the next year, not the entire map. Just the next faithful yes. Over time, you'll look back and realize He was drawing a beautiful line with your small steps.

Reflection Question: What's your next faithful step—even if you can't see the whole path?

Day 12

"And they that know thy name will put their trust in thee: for thou, LORD, hast not forsaken them that seek thee." — Psalm 9:10 (KJV)

Trust grows where knowledge deepens. The more you know God's name—His character—the easier it is to place your weight on Him. He doesn't forsake seekers. Not the exhausted ones, not the doubting ones, not the coming-back-again ones. Think of a sturdy chair: the first time you sit, you test it. After a while, you sit without thinking. God has held you before. He'll hold you again. Let your memory preach: "He didn't forsake me then; He won't now."

Reflection Question: Which name of God do you need to lean on most today—and why?

Day 13

"Now the God of hope fill you with all joy and peace in believing..." — Romans 15:13a (KJV)

Hope has a Source, and He's generous. Joy and peace don't come as prizes after perfect faith; they come as gifts while you're believing. Picture God pouring into your cup—a steady stream that doesn't depend on the weather of your life. Believing is the open cup. Closed hands can't receive. If cynicism has crusted over your hope, ask Him to soften it. He delights to fill what you bring, even if it feels small. In believing, joy and peace rise like warm bread in the oven—quiet, steady, fragrant.

Reflection Question: Where will you hold your cup open today for God's hope to fill?

Day 14

"Come unto me, all ye that labour and are heavy laden, and I will give you rest." — Matthew 11:28 (KJV)

Jesus doesn't say, "Clean up and then come." He says, "Come as you are, burdened and tired." Rest is not a reward for finishing your list; it's a gift for bringing your load to Him. Picture setting down a heavy backpack you've carried too long—responsibility, regret, expectations. His rest isn't just a nap; it's a soul-deep ease that comes from being loved, held, and unhurried by heaven. You can breathe again. You don't have to carry everything by yourself.

Reflection Question: What burden will you bring to Jesus today so He can give you rest?

Day 15

"Fear thou not; for I am with thee..." — Isaiah 41:10a (KJV)

God doesn't say there's nothing to fear; He says you're not alone in it. His with-ness changes the math. Like a child who sleeps better when someone sits by the bed, your heart steadies when you realize He is here. He strengthens, helps, upholds. He doesn't outsource your care. When fear starts writing scripts—"What if?" "What then?"—let His presence be the louder line: "I am with you." Courage isn't the absence of trembling; it's the presence of God in the trembling.

Reflection Question: How will you remind yourself today that God is with you right now?

Day 16

"The LORD is my shepherd; I shall not want." — Psalm 23:1 (KJV)

A shepherd leads, feeds, protects, and stays. That's the picture David paints—and he makes it personal: my Shepherd. Not distant. Not distracted. Yours. Lack loses its loudness when the Shepherd is near. He knows the green pastures your soul needs and the still waters that quiet your mind. He knows the valley path too, and He doesn't rush you through it. You may not have everything you want, but with Him, you will not lack what you truly need.

Reflection Question: Where do you need to follow your Shepherd's lead instead of your hurry?

Day 17

"If any of you lack wisdom, let him ask of God... and it shall be given him." — James 1:5 (KJV)

God doesn't roll His eyes at your questions. He gives wisdom without scolding. When choices pile up—school schedules, medical options, boundaries with family—ask. Wisdom isn't just information; it's insight shaped by God's heart. He knows how to weave truth and love, timing and tone. Expect guidance to come in layers: a verse that stands out, a nudge in prayer, wise counsel from a friend, holy common sense. He loves to lead you.

Reflection Question: What decision needs God's wisdom, and how will you pause to ask Him?

Day 18

"It is of the LORD'S mercies that we are not consumed, because his compassions fail not." — Lamentations 3:22 (KJV)

Some mornings, mercy feels like coffee for your soul—warm, steadying, new. God's compassion doesn't run out like the last drop in the pot. When yesterday's mistakes echo, His mercy answers louder. You are not consumed by what could have been or should have been because His faithful love holds today. Start again, not by trying harder, but by trusting His never-failing heart toward you. Mercy meets you where you are and gently moves you forward.

Reflection Question: Where do you need to receive fresh mercy and let yesterday be yesterday?

Day 19

"Casting all your care upon him; for he careth for you." — 1 Peter 5:7 (KJV)

Cares pile up like laundry—small ones, big ones, hidden ones. God invites you to toss them onto Him, not fold and carry them yourself. Casting isn't polite; it's honest. "Here, Lord. This too." His care is not theoretical. It's personal and present. He's not tired of your repeated concerns. He's a Father who bends low to listen, then stands strong to carry. The lighter shoulders you feel aren't irresponsibility; they're trust at work.

Reflection Question: What's one specific care you will cast on God instead of carrying today?

Day 20

"Commit thy works unto the LORD, and thy thoughts shall be established." — Proverbs 16:3 (KJV)

When your to-do list feels like a runaway cart, commit your work to God. Not just the churchy things—the emails, the spreadsheets, the meal prep, the carpool. Invite Him into it all. As you do, your thoughts settle. Clarity grows where chaos lived. You remember why you're doing what you're doing and for Whom. Even interruptions become holy assignments under His hand. Work becomes worship, and worry loses its bite.

Reflection Question: How can you dedicate today's tasks to the Lord before you begin?

Day 21

"O taste and see that the LORD is good: blessed is the man that trusteth in him." — Psalm 34:8 (KJV)

God invites you to taste, not just read the menu. Trust is the bite. Sometimes we wait to feel certain before we step—but tasting comes first. Try the prayer. Make the call. Forgive the hurt. As you act on His goodness, you'll see more of it. Blessing isn't a vague halo; it's the deep wellbeing of a heart resting in a good God. Even hard days have flavor when you notice His kindness sprinkled through them.

Reflection Question: What small "taste" of trust will you try today to experience God's goodness?

Day 22

"Peace I leave with you, my peace I give unto you..." — John 14:27a (KJV)

Jesus doesn't loan peace; He gives it. And not just any peace—His peace. The kind that held steady in storms and on long, hard days. The world's peace depends on calm circumstances; His peace depends on a faithful Savior. Receive it like you would a warm blanket on a chilly morning. Let it cover your anxious places. You don't earn this peace; you accept it and make space for it—slow breaths, Scripture in your ears, His name on your lips.

Reflection Question: What helps you make space to receive the peace Jesus is giving today?

Day 23

"When thou passest through the waters, I will be with thee..." — Isaiah 43:2a (KJV)

God doesn't promise you'll avoid deep waters; He promises presence in them. The river may be a diagnosis, a transition, or a stack of bills. Waters rise, but they won't have the final word. His nearness is your life jacket. You might come out wet and wiser, but you will not be washed away. Look for Him in the small mercies—timely help, a friend's text, an unexpected calm. Those are evidence of the One walking you through.

Reflection Question: Where have you seen signs of God's presence in your "waters" lately?

Day 24

"If ye have faith as a grain of mustard seed... nothing shall be impossible unto you." — Matthew 17:20b (KJV)

Mustard-seed faith is tiny, but living. It grows. God isn't asking for giant faith; He's inviting living faith—real, planted, entrusted. Put that small seed in His big hands. Speak to the mountain—maybe it's bitterness, procrastination, or fear—and take the next obedient step. Mountains move in inches and in miracles. Don't despise slow. Every inch is grace, every step a testimony: God is working with my little yes.

Reflection Question: What is one "mustard-seed" step you can take toward a stubborn mountain?

Day 25

"My help cometh from the LORD, which made heaven and earth." — Psalm 121:2 (KJV)

Your Helper is the Maker. The One who spoke galaxies into place isn't stumped by your calendar or your challenges. When you feel underqualified or outnumbered, lift your eyes. Help doesn't always arrive as instant fixes; sometimes it's stamina, wisdom, or a holy no. Expect practical help from a powerful God—strength to show up, grace to let go, courage to ask for support. You're not bothering Him. You're honoring Him by depending on Him.

Reflection Question: Where do you need to lift your eyes and ask the Maker for help today?

Day 26

"The name of the LORD is a strong tower: the righteous runneth into it, and is safe." — Proverbs 18:10 (KJV)

When threats feel close—criticism, temptation, bad news—run to His name. Not to distraction, not to numbing, not to over-explaining. His name is His character—faithful, holy, healer, provider. Picture a tower: thick walls, a sturdy door, a high view. Safety doesn't mean the storm stops; it means the storm doesn't own you. Inside His name, you can breathe, pray, and see with perspective. Running to Him is wisdom, not weakness.

Reflection Question: Which name of God will you "run into" as your strong tower today?

Day 27

"Trust in him at all times; ye people, pour out your heart before him: God is a refuge for us. Selah." — Psalm 62:8 (KJV)

"All times" includes the messy middles—when results are pending, when emotions are mixed, when nothing is tidy. God invites your whole heart, not a curated version. Pour out like water, not like a slow drip. Then rest in the refuge of being fully known and fully loved. Selah—pause and let it sink in. You can trust Him in the morning confidence and the midnight questions. He holds both.

Reflection Question: What unfiltered thing do you need to say to God and then pause?

Day 28

"Let us hold fast the profession of our faith without wavering; (for he is faithful that promised;)" — Hebrews 10:23 (KJV)

Your grip might feel weak, but the One you're holding is faithful. Holding fast isn't clenching in panic; it's refusing to trade truth for convenience or fear. Remember what He promised, and remember who promised. His track record is flawless. When doubts tap your shoulder, answer with His faithfulness—stories of His past provision, Scriptures that don't crack under weight, songs that steadied you before. Keep your confession clear: God is faithful.

Reflection Question: What promise of God will you rehearse to steady your grip today?

Day 29

"In the world ye shall have tribulation: but be of good cheer; I have overcome the world." — John 16:33b (KJV)

Jesus is honest: troubles are real. He's also victorious: He has overcome. Good cheer isn't denial; it's defiance—a smile that says, "My Savior wins." When headlines are heavy and personal news is harder, anchor to His victory. It's not just future hope; it's present courage. The Overcomer lives in you. That means you can face this day with a lifted chin and a settled heart.

Reflection Question: Where can you practice courageous cheer because Jesus has overcome?

Day 30

"I had fainted, unless I had believed to see the goodness of the LORD in the land of the living." — Psalm 27:13 (KJV)

Belief keeps you from fainting. Not blind belief, but belief anchored in God's goodness here and now—"in the land of the living." Look for goodness like a treasure hunter: a text at the right time, a parking spot on a hard day, a laugh that loosens your shoulders. These aren't small; they're breadcrumbs of a good God. Let them fuel your hope for bigger things you can't yet see.

Reflection Question: What evidence of God's goodness can you spot in your life today?

Day 31

"The LORD is good, a strong hold in the day of trouble; and he knoweth them that trust in him." — Nahum 1:7 (KJV)

God's goodness isn't seasonal. On the sunniest days and the stormiest ones, He remains a strong hold. He also knows you—your story, your struggles, your stubborn places, your faith that keeps showing up. Being known by Him is safety all its own. When trouble knocks, let His goodness be the door you open first. Run to the One who knows exactly how to hold you and what to do next.

Reflection Question: How will you lean into God's goodness as your strong hold today?

February: Love and Compassion

Day 32

"We love him, because he first loved us." — 1 John 4:19 (KJV)

God made the first move. Before you cleaned up your act or figured out your faith, love stepped toward you. That changes how we love others. We're not trying to earn anything; we're responding to everything. Think of a porch light left on—welcoming you home, even when you're late. His love is like that: steady, patient, warm. When you're tired or short-fused, remember the Source. You don't have to manufacture love like a product; you receive it like sunlight and then share the warmth. His love is not a feeling that fades with the weather; it's a foundation you can stand on, especially on messy days.

Reflection Question: Where can you respond to God's first love by taking the first gracious step toward someone today?

Day 33

"A new commandment I give unto you, That ye love one another; as I have loved you..." — John 13:34 (KJV)

"As I have loved you" raises the bar. Not "as you feel" or "as they deserve," but as Jesus loves—steady, sacrificial, with sleeves rolled up. Love looks like answering the late text, listening without fixing, dropping off soup, or holding your tongue. It's not flashy; it's faithful. Imagine your home, church, or workplace as a garden. Love is the daily watering—small, consistent acts that keep hearts from drying out. People recognize Jesus in that kind of care. You don't need a big platform to love big; you need a willing heart and the courage to go first.

Reflection Question: Who can you love "as Jesus loves" through one small, faithful act today?

Day 34

"Charity suffereth long, and is kind..." — 1 Corinthians 13:4 (KJV)

Love has a long fuse and soft hands. Patience and kindness together are powerful. Anyone can be kind for a minute; real love keeps showing up when the wait drags on and the nerves wear thin. Think of long lines at the grocery store—kindness offers a smile to the frazzled cashier and patience keeps it genuine when the line doesn't move. In relationships, patience gives breathing room; kindness fills that space with gentleness. You may not control timelines or outcomes, but you can choose tone and tenderness. Long-suffering isn't weakness; it's strength under the Spirit's control.

Reflection Question: Where can you pair patience with kindness in a situation that's testing you?

Day 35

"And be ye kind one to another, tenderhearted, forgiving one another, even as God for Christ's sake hath forgiven you." — Ephesians 4:32 (KJV)

Kindness is love's everyday outfit. Tenderhearted means your heart stays soft, not guarded by grudges. Forgiveness is how softness survives real life. You're not pretending it didn't hurt; you're choosing not to chain yourself to it. God didn't forgive you because you earned it; He forgave because Jesus paid it. That frees you to release others from the debts you keep tallying in your head. Forgiveness may not rebuild trust overnight, but it unclenches your fist so you can heal. Sometimes the kindest thing you do is drop the invisible scorecard.

Reflection Question: What offense can you loosen your grip on today, remembering how God has forgiven you?

Day 36

"Put on therefore... bowels of mercies, kindness, humbleness of mind, meekness, longsuffering." — Colossians 3:12 (KJV)

"Put on" suggests choice. Like picking a sweater on a chilly morning, you can choose compassion when the day starts. Mercy warms cold spaces—at home, in the office, in your own thoughts. Humility admits you don't know the whole story. Meekness isn't timid; it's strength that refuses to bulldoze. Longsuffering means you stay kind when the wait stretches. Picture compassion as a coat you wear into every room; you change the temperature just by entering. God isn't asking you to feel perfectly loving—He's inviting you to dress your attitude in His character.

Reflection Question: What "compassion coat" will you put on before you step into your next conversation?

Day 37

"But God commendeth his love toward us, in that, while we were yet sinners, Christ died for us." — Romans 5:8 (KJV)

God didn't wait for you to get it together. He loved you in the middle of your mess and moved toward you with a cross. That kind of love loosens shame's grip and reshapes how we treat others mid-story. When someone disappoints you, it's tempting to withdraw love like a canceled subscription. God did the opposite with you. His love is proof, not theory. Let that sink deep: you are fully seen and fully loved. Out of that security, compassion becomes less a chore and more a natural overflow.

Reflection Question: Who needs you to move toward them with grace, the way God moved toward you?

Day 38

"Let not mercy and truth forsake thee: bind them about thy neck; write them upon the table of thine heart." — Proverbs 3:3 (KJV)

Mercy and truth are a beautiful pair—like a necklace you never take off and words etched where you can't forget. Mercy without truth gets mushy; truth without mercy gets sharp. Together, they make love both safe and strong. In a hard talk, mercy chooses a gentle tone; truth speaks clearly. In self-talk, mercy quiets shame; truth corrects lies. Wear both into your day. Let your words fit like jewelry—adding grace, not weight. And let your heart carry God's steady truth so your compassion has roots, not just feelings.

Reflection Question: Where do you need to blend mercy with truth so love stays both kind and clear?

Day 39

"Be ye therefore merciful, as your Father also is merciful." — Luke 6:36 (KJV)

Mercy looks like not returning the jab, like giving the benefit of the doubt, like choosing a gentle reply when sarcasm would land better in the moment. Your Father is merciful—He knows your frame, remembers you're dust, and meets you with compassion. When we copy Him, homes soften and hearts exhale. Mercy isn't letting harmful patterns continue unchecked; it's coming with a redemptive posture, not a gotcha spirit. Start with how God treats you on your worst days—and let that shape how you treat others on theirs.

Reflection Question: What moment today could be transformed by answering with mercy instead of reacting?

Day 40

"Look not every man on his own things, but every man also on the things of others." — Philippians 2:4 (KJV)

Love looks up. It lifts its eyes from the calendar and catches needs right in front of it. Not because your stuff doesn't matter, but because God multiplies time when we live open-handed. Think of holding a door, remembering a name, sending a quick "thinking of you" text. Small? Sure. But small love often carries the heaviest weight. Jesus noticed people others walked past. Compassion begins with attention. When you look up, you'll spot assignments God tucked into ordinary minutes.

Reflection Question: Whose "things" can you thoughtfully notice and care for in a small way today?

Day 41

"And above all things have fervent charity among yourselves: for charity shall cover the multitude of sins." — 1 Peter 4:8 (KJV)

Love doesn't excuse sin, but it covers—like a warm blanket over a cold night. Fervent love is active, not lukewarm. It chooses to protect a reputation instead of rehearsing a failure. It believes the best where it can and confronts wisely where it must. In families and friendships, covering looks like refusing to gossip, guarding confidences, and giving room for growth. When you've been covered by someone else's grace, you know how healing it feels. That's a love worth passing on.

Reflection Question: Where can your love "cover" instead of expose, healing instead of highlighting a fault?

Day 42

"My little children, let us not love in word, neither in tongue; but in deed and in truth." — 1 John 3:18 (KJV)

Words matter, but actions make them believable. "Let me know if you need anything" is kind; showing up with dinner or childcare is love with shoes on. Deed and truth together mean our help is both practical and honest. We don't enable harm, but we do enter the struggle. Love is the ride to the appointment, the bill split, the text that says, "I'm outside—come walk." It's ordinary faithfulness that adds up to extraordinary care.

Reflection Question: What tangible deed can turn your kind words into real help for someone today?

Day 43

"But the fruit of the Spirit is love, joy, peace, longsuffering, gentleness, goodness, faith," — Galatians 5:22 (KJV)

Fruit grows where roots are healthy. You can't staple apples to a branch and call it an orchard. Love that lasts doesn't come from trying harder; it comes from staying connected to the Spirit. As you abide, He produces what you can't manufacture—joy that outlasts moods, peace that outlasts headlines, patience that outlasts long lines. The pressure eases: you don't have to be the source. You're the branch. He's faithful to grow what He plants.

Reflection Question: How will you stay connected to the Spirit today so love can naturally grow?

Day 44

"Thou shalt love the Lord thy God... And... Thou shalt love thy neighbour as thyself." — Matthew 22:37, 39 (KJV)

Jesus simplifies what we complicate: love God; love people. Loving God anchors you; loving people proves it. Loving yourself rightly matters too—it's hard to love neighbors when your inner talk is cruel. Let God's love redefine your worth, then let that worth spill outward. Picture three directions: up (worship), in (healthy grace), out (kindness). When these lines connect, your life draws a clear picture of God's heart in everyday ways—at the sink, in meetings, on the phone.

Reflection Question: Which direction—up, in, or out—needs attention so your love stays balanced today?

Day 45

"Who comforteth us in all our tribulation, that we may be able to comfort them which are in any trouble..." — *2 Corinthians 1:4 (KJV)*

Your tears are not wasted; they're training you to be gentle. The comfort God gave you becomes a toolkit for someone else. You don't need perfect words—often, presence is the gift. Sit on the couch. Bring the coffee. Share the story of how God met you in your own valley. That's not making it about you; it's opening a window so hope can blow in. The comfort cycle keeps moving: God to you, you to others, all pointing back to Him.

Reflection Question: Who could use the same comfort God once gave you—and how might you offer it?

Day 46

"Let brotherly love continue. Be not forgetful to entertain strangers: for thereby some have entertained angels unawares." — *Hebrews 13:1-2 (KJV)*

Hospitality is love with a spare chair. It doesn't require a magazine-perfect house—just a welcome. A pot of soup, a cleared corner table, a porch visit count. Scripture hints that ordinary welcomes may brush the edge of heaven. That neighbor you barely know, the new face at church, the coworker who always eats alone—love sees them and makes room. You might be the safe place someone's been praying for.

Reflection Question: What simple invitation could turn your space into a refuge for someone this week?

Day 47

"But a certain Samaritan... when he saw him, he had compassion on him," — Luke 10:33 (KJV)

Compassion starts with seeing. The priest and Levite saw and crossed the street; the Samaritan saw and crossed the gap. Love moves toward messes—bloody knees, complicated stories, inconvenient timing. It costs something: time, money, emotional energy. But it also changes everything. When you've been the one in the ditch, you know how holy a lifted hand feels. Ask God for Samaritan eyes today—eyes that notice, feet that move, hands that help.

Reflection Question: Where might God be inviting you to cross the street and turn pity into action?

Day 48

"Pure religion and undefiled before God and the Father is this, To visit the fatherless and widows in their affliction..." — James 1:27 (KJV)

God's heart bends toward the vulnerable. Ours can too—in practical, local ways. "Visit" is personal. It's showing up, not just signing up. Maybe it's supporting a foster family, checking on a widow down the block, mentoring a teen, or giving to a ministry that serves quietly. You don't have to fix everything; you can faithfully love someone. Pure religion looks like presence that doesn't rush away when stories get heavy.

Reflection Question: Who in your world is vulnerable, and what small presence can you offer them?

Day 49

"Blessed are the merciful: for they shall obtain mercy." — Matthew 5:7 (KJV)

Mercy is boomerang blessing. When you send it out, it has a way of returning—sometimes from unexpected places, always from God. Being merciful doesn't mean being a doormat; it means choosing compassion when you could choose payback. Think of the last time someone cut you slack—you breathed easier, right? You can be that breath for someone else. And when your turn comes to need mercy (it will), God promises you won't find an empty shelf.

Reflection Question: Where can you offer mercy today, trusting God to refill what you pour out?

Day 50

"The LORD is gracious, and full of compassion; slow to anger, and of great mercy." — Psalm 145:8 (KJV)

God is not quick-tempered with you. He is rich in compassion, not stingy. Let that recalibrate how you think about Him—and how you respond to others. When tempers flare, slow is holy. Compassion pauses, asks a question, softens a tone. You reflect the Father's heart when you choose grace over the last word. If you struggle with a short fuse, you're not stuck; His compassion toward you becomes the model and the power for change in you.

Reflection Question: How can you mirror God's slowness to anger in a tense moment today?

Day 51

"The LORD thy God in the midst of thee is mighty... he will rejoice over thee with singing." — Zephaniah 3:17 (KJV)

Imagine God singing over you—your name in a love song. Not because you nailed the day, but because you're His. That kind of love brings courage. When you walk into a room, you're not auditioning; you're already beloved. Loved people love well. You can celebrate others instead of competing, cheer instead of compare. God's melody in your soul quiets the noisy lies and frees you to pour joy on someone else's life.

Reflection Question: What's one way you can "sing over" someone today with encouragement or celebration?

Day 52

"The LORD is nigh unto them that are of a broken heart..." — Psalm 34:18 (KJV)

Broken hearts feel lonely, but they aren't. God draws near to the cracked places. He doesn't hurry you along or slap on platitudes. He sits with you, like a friend who knows how to hold silence. If you're grieving, His nearness is your oxygen. If someone you love is hurting, your nearness can echo His—slow, gentle, present. You don't have to fix the pain to be a faithful companion through it.

Reflection Question: Who needs your quiet nearness today, and how can you offer it without trying to fix?

Day 53

"Be kindly affectioned one to another with brotherly love; in honour preferring one another;" — Romans 12:10 (KJV)

Honoring others looks like letting someone else go first, giving the bigger piece, choosing words that add dignity. It's the opposite of one-up stories and elbowing for the spotlight. In a world that rewards loud, love can be different—gentle, honoring, unhurried. When you prefer another, you don't disappear; you display Jesus. Watch how room opens up—for them and for you. God has a way of lifting those who lift others.

Reflection Question: What simple choice can you make today that puts someone else first with joy?

Day 54

"Rejoice with them that do rejoice, and weep with them that weep." — Romans 12:15 (KJV)

Love knows how to match the room. It throws confetti at the promotion and brings tissues to the setback. Sometimes it's easier to weep than to rejoice—or vice versa—depending on your season. Ask God for a flexible heart that can celebrate without envy and lament without fixing. Shared joy doubles; shared sorrow halves. Both are holy. Your presence in someone's moment tells them, "You're not alone," and that is gospel-shaped comfort.

Reflection Question: Who can you celebrate or sit beside today so they feel truly accompanied?

Day 55

"This is my commandment, That ye love one another, as I have loved you. Greater love hath no man than this, that a man lay down his life for his friends." — John 15:12-13 (KJV)

Love costs. It might not look like a heroic rescue; it often looks like laying down your schedule, your right to be right, your comfort. Jesus set the standard by laying down His life. When you lay something down for someone else, you echo Him. It's the ride to the airport at 5 a.m., the last slice given away, the apology offered first. These small deaths make room for resurrection life in relationships.

Reflection Question: What could you lay down today so love can take up more space?

Day 56

"He hath shewed thee... what doth the LORD require of thee, but to do justly, and to love mercy, and to walk humbly with thy God?" — Micah 6:8 (KJV)

Justice, mercy, humility—a three-beat rhythm for a life of love. Do justly: act fairly in small choices—tips, time, truth. Love mercy: delight in second chances, for yourself and others. Walk humbly: stay teachable, close to God, willing to say "I was wrong." When these beats sync, compassion has both backbone and softness. You don't have to solve every headline; you can live this out on your street, in your workplace, in your home.

Reflection Question: Which beat—justice, mercy, or humility—needs turning up in your life today?

Day 57

"Take my yoke upon you, and learn of me; for I am meek and lowly in heart..." — *Matthew 11:29 (KJV)*

Jesus invites you to learn His gentleness. Meekness isn't being quiet at all costs; it's power under love's guidance. Picture two oxen in a yoke—walking together keeps the load steady. When you match pace with Jesus, He teaches you a way of loving that is firm but not harsh, honest but not hurtful. The more you learn His heart, the less you need to prove yours. Gentleness becomes your go-to, even when tensions rise.

Reflection Question: How can you match Jesus' gentle pace in a relationship that easily gets tense?

Day 58

"The desire of a man is his kindness: and a poor man is better than a liar." — *Proverbs 19:22 (KJV)*

What people most value isn't polish—it's kindness. We remember how someone made us feel far longer than we remember their résumé. Kindness is affordable and priceless at the same time. You can be low on cash or capacity and still be generous with your tone, your patience, your smile. God values truth and kindness over image and impressiveness. In a culture chasing shiny, love chooses genuine.

Reflection Question: What ordinary kindness can you offer today that money can't buy?

Day 59

"Beloved, if God so loved us, we ought also to love one another." — 1 John 4:11 (KJV)

Start with "Beloved." That's your name in God's mouth. Loved people become loving people—not perfectly, but genuinely. "Ought" here isn't a heavy sigh; it's a natural next step. If God's love reached you at your worst, it can flow through you to others at theirs. You're not the reservoir; you're the riverbed. Let His love run through your ordinary routes—errands, texts, meetings, mealtimes—and watch how even routine days glimmer.

Reflection Question: What relationship could change if you approached it first as "Beloved," then as "giver of love"?

Leap Day Bonus

"And above all these things put on charity, which is the bond of perfectness." — Colossians 3:14 (KJV)

Love is the belt that holds everything together. Gifts, talents, goals—they're good, but without love they don't fit right. "Put on" suggests intention. On a leap day, when the calendar surprises you with extra space, consider love as the extra you choose to add. A little more patience. A little more listening. A little more celebration of someone else's win. Love binds scattered pieces into a whole that feels like Jesus.

Reflection Question: What extra measure of love can you "put on" today to hold your world together in Christ?

MARCH: RENEWAL AND GROWTH

Day 60

"They are new every morning: great is thy faithfulness." —
Lamentations 3:23 (KJV)

Mornings come with mercy baked in. Before your feet hit the floor, God has already refilled your cup. New doesn't always mean dramatic; sometimes it's a fresh start in the same kitchen, with the same people, and a heart made softer by grace. Think of wiping a foggy mirror—suddenly, you can see again. That's what His faithfulness does after a long night of worry or regret. You're allowed to start over, not because you ignored yesterday, but because God's compassion outlasted it. Today can hold new patterns, kinder words, and braver steps because He's steady, and His steadiness becomes your strength.

Reflection Question: Where do you need to receive today as a true new start from God's faithful heart?

Day 61

"Behold, I will do a new thing; now it shall spring forth; shall ye not know it?" — Isaiah 43:19a (KJV)

God loves surprising us with green shoots in dry places. New jobs, new friendships, new courage—sometimes they begin as tiny sprouts you could miss if you're only watching for big breakthroughs. Think of early spring: bare branches suddenly dotted with buds. Renewal often starts quietly. Pay attention to small shifts—an old fear losing volume, a fresh desire to pray, an idea that won't leave you alone. God is not stuck, and you're not either. He makes roads in deserts and rivers through the stuck parts of our souls.

Reflection Question: What small "bud" of newness do you see God growing—and how will you nurture it?

Day 62

"Therefore if any man be in Christ, he is a new creature: old things are passed away; behold, all things are become new." — 2 Corinthians 5:17 (KJV)

In Christ, you're not just upgraded—you're made new. The old story doesn't own you anymore. That doesn't mean every habit vanishes overnight, but the core has changed. Picture moving into a renovated home: the address is the same, but the inside is different—light where there was darkness, space where there was clutter. When the past knocks, you don't have to answer as the person you were. Growth is learning to live like the new you—choosing forgiveness over bitterness, truth over old lies, hope over cynicism—one decision, one room at a time.

Reflection Question: Which "old thing" will you refuse to live in today because you're new in Christ?

Day 63

"Be ye transformed by the renewing of your mind..." — Romans 12:2b (KJV)

Transformation begins where your thoughts live. Renewal is like swapping out old playlists that keep you anxious for a new soundtrack of God's truth. Over time, what you rehearse becomes how you respond. Think of repainting a room—first the primer, then steady coats. Scripture is the primer; daily choices are the coats. Soon, the atmosphere changes. You can't always change what happens, but you can let God change how you think about it, which changes how you walk through it. Little by little, your mind learns a new way home.

Reflection Question: What thought will you replace today with a truth that helps you breathe and believe?

Day 64

"I am the vine, ye are the branches... for without me ye can do nothing." — John 15:5 (KJV)

Growth is not gritting your teeth—it's staying connected. A branch doesn't strain to produce grapes; it abides and fruit shows up. Your job is not to manufacture results but to stay close to Jesus: talk with Him, listen for Him, walk with Him. Think of charging your phone overnight—connection brings power you can't drum up on your own. When you feel drained, don't try harder; plug in deeper. Fruit—love, joy, peace—comes from His life flowing through yours.

Reflection Question: How will you "abide" practically today so His life can flow into your ordinary moments?

Day 65

"And he shall be like a tree planted by the rivers of water... his leaf also shall not wither." — Psalm 1:3 (KJV)

Planted people flourish. Not because life is easy, but because their roots are near water. Planting looks like rhythms that keep you close to God—Scripture in your ears on the commute, prayer while folding laundry, worship on a walk. When heat comes, you don't dry up as fast, because your source isn't the weather—it's the river. Leaves may get windblown, but they won't wither. You can be steady in a shaky world when your roots drink deeply from Him.

Reflection Question: What daily rhythm could deepen your roots beside God's river this week?

Day 66

"He shall come unto us as the rain, as the latter and former rain unto the earth." — Hosea 6:3b (KJV)

Rain is gentle and persistent. It soaks the hard ground slowly, then suddenly everything is green. God's presence refreshes like that—some days a soft drizzle, other days a soaking storm of kindness. Dry seasons happen, but they aren't permanent. Keep your heart turned upward. Open places: worship, Scripture, community. Rain finds cracks. One day you'll notice new color in places you thought were done growing. That's His faithfulness, arriving right on time.

Reflection Question: Where do you need to lift your face to God's "rain" and let Him soften a hard place?

Day 67

"He which hath begun a good work in you will perform it until the day of Jesus Christ." — Philippians 1:6 (KJV)

God is not a starter who doesn't finish. He began good in you, and He's committed to completing it. Progress may feel slow—a step forward, two sideways, one back—but the Builder stays on site. Think of a renovation with dust everywhere; it looks worse before it looks better. Don't mistake the mess for failure. The plan is still unfolding. You are God's workmanship, and He doesn't abandon projects He loves.

Reflection Question: What sign of God's ongoing work can you spot, even if the process feels messy?

Day 68

"A new heart also will I give you, and a new spirit will I put within you..." — Ezekiel 36:26a (KJV)

God doesn't patch the old heart; He gives a new one. That matters on days you feel stuck in the same reactions. New heart means new capacity—soft where you were hard, brave where you were fearful, tender where you were numb. Imagine swapping a cracked, leaky cup for one that can actually hold water. You're not doomed to spill grace; the Spirit helps you hold it. Growth begins with believing what He's already placed inside you.

Reflection Question: Where will you act from your new heart today instead of your old habits?

Day 69

"...let us lay aside every weight... and let us run with patience the race that is set before us," — Hebrews 12:1 (KJV)

Growth sometimes looks like subtraction. Not every weight is a sin; some are just heavy. Expectations, comparisons, clutter—good things that slow your pace. Picture a runner dropping a backpack before the race. Freedom feels lighter than you remember. Patience sets the pace; you're not sprinting someone else's course. You have your race, your lane, your assignment. Lay aside what drags, and keep a steady, grace-filled stride.

Reflection Question: What weight can you release so you can run your race with a lighter heart?

Day 70

"And let us not be weary in well doing: for in due season we shall reap, if we faint not." — Galatians 6:9 (KJV)

Doing good can feel thankless—packing lunches, serving quietly, staying faithful when no one notices. But seeds are buried before they're beautiful. Due season is real. It might not match your calendar, but God keeps time perfectly. Think of a garden—dirt looks empty, yet life is happening underground. Keep watering. Keep showing up. Tired doesn't mean you're failing; it means you're investing. Harvest comes to the faithful, not the flashy.

Reflection Question: Where do you need to keep watering a hidden seed, trusting God for due season?

Day 71

"They that wait upon the LORD shall renew their strength..." — Isaiah 40:31a (KJV)

Waiting feels like sitting in a stalled line, tapping the steering wheel. But waiting on the Lord isn't idle; it's trusting. As you look to Him, strength gets swapped—your exhaustion for His endurance. Like plugging in a drained battery, renewal happens while you're still. Wings grow where weariness was. You'll run again. You'll walk without quitting. The timeline may be unclear, but the promise is not: renewal meets those who wait with hope.

Reflection Question: How can you turn your waiting into worship so strength can quietly return?

Day 72

"Create in me a clean heart, O God; and renew a right spirit within me." — Psalm 51:10 (KJV)

There's a prayer God loves to answer: make me new inside. A clean heart isn't squeaky perfection; it's an honest heart that keeps short accounts. When resentment builds or motives muddle, invite God to scrub the corners. Think dishwater turning clear as fresh water flows in. Renewal happens where confession meets compassion. You walk lighter, freer, less tangled in yourself—and more available to love others well.

Reflection Question: What corner of your heart needs God's cleansing so your spirit can be renewed?

Day 73

"...the new man, which is renewed in knowledge after the image of him that created him." — Colossians 3:10 (KJV)

You're being remade to look like your Creator—piece by piece, choice by choice. Renewal in knowledge means learning Jesus and letting that learning change you. Not facts alone, but familiarity. Like living with someone and picking up their phrases, you start sounding like Him—more patient, more truthful, more brave. The goal isn't a curated image; it's His image, quietly shining through everyday you.

Reflection Question: What about Jesus do you want to know better so you can reflect Him more clearly?

Day 74

"But grow in grace, and in the knowledge of our Lord and Saviour Jesus Christ." — 2 Peter 3:18 (KJV)

Growth in grace is not a sprint; it's a lifetime of small inches. Think sourdough starter—feed it consistently, and it rises. Starve it, and it slumps. Grace grows as you keep coming to Jesus, receiving what you can't earn, and passing it along. Knowledge grows too—not to puff up, but to build up. You can be both soft and strong, rooted and reaching. Keep feeding the starter. Rise again.

Reflection Question: What small "feeding" will help grace rise in you today?

Day 75

"And other fell on good ground, and did yield fruit... and increased;
and brought forth..." — Mark 4:8 (KJV)

Good ground isn't glamorous; it's receptive. It listens, holds, and makes space for seeds to do what seeds do. You can't control the rain or the sun, but you can tend the soil—pull the weeds of distraction, break up hard places with humility, water with consistent truth. Fruit comes in time, and increase follows health. You don't need to mimic someone else's field. Let God cultivate yours.

Reflection Question: What "soil work" can you do so God's Word has room to take root and grow?

Day 76

"Except a corn of wheat fall into the ground and die, it abideth alone:
but if it die, it bringeth forth much fruit." — John 12:24 (KJV)

Some growth requires letting something die—an old expectation, a prideful stance, a habit that kept you safe but small. Burials feel final, but in God's hands they're beginnings. The seed disappears before the green appears. Think of pruning a rosebush; cutting back looks harsh, but blooms multiply. Trust the Gardener. What feels like loss may be the doorway to your most fruitful season yet.

Reflection Question: What needs to be surrendered so new life can break through in you?

Day 77

"For a just man falleth seven times, and riseth up again..." — Proverbs 24:16a (KJV)

Rising is part of righteousness. Growth isn't never falling; it's refusing to stay down. Picture a toddler learning to walk—wobbly, determined, cheered on. God's not tallying tumbles; He's celebrating your getting up. When shame wants to glue you to the floor, grace offers a hand. Try again. Adjust your footing. Learn from what tripped you. Up you go—by His strength, for His glory.

Reflection Question: Where do you need to get up one more time and take another step?

Day 78

"Now unto him that is able to do exceeding abundantly above all that we ask or think..." — Ephesians 3:20 (KJV)

God's capacity outruns your imagination. Renewal doesn't stop at "good enough"; it often spills into more than you asked for. You prayed for patience, and He grew compassion. You hoped for a door, and He gave a pathway. This isn't about getting everything you want—it's about watching a generous God write better stories than you knew to request. Keep asking. Keep trusting. Leave room for "above."

Reflection Question: Where can you expect God's "above and beyond" without scripting how it must look?

Day 79

"The righteous shall flourish like the palm tree... They shall still bring forth fruit in old age." — Psalm 92:12, 14 (KJV)

Palms bend without breaking. That's flourish. Age doesn't cancel fruitfulness; it refines it. Seasons shift—from sprinting to steady mentoring, from busy hands to wise words—but fruit remains. Your roots in God make you weatherproof. Even when strength changes, significance doesn't. There's fresh sap for you yet—new encouragement to pour, prayers to plant, wisdom to share. Flourishing isn't a decade; it's a rooted life.

Reflection Question: What fruit can you offer in this season that fits your current strength and wisdom?

Day 80

"Count it all joy when ye fall into divers temptations; knowing this, that the trying of your faith worketh patience." — James 1:2-3 (KJV)

Joy in trials sounds upside down until you notice what hardship grows. Patience. Depth. Steadiness. Like muscles after resistance training, your faith fibers strengthen under pressure. You wouldn't choose the weight, but you can welcome the growth. Joy doesn't mean enjoying pain; it means valuing the outcome. God wastes nothing—not even the hard set you didn't want to lift.

Reflection Question: How might this current challenge be strengthening something in you worth keeping?

Day 81

"Be ye stedfast, unmoveable, always abounding in the work of the Lord... your labour is not in vain in the Lord." — 1 Corinthians 15:58 (KJV)

Abounding and steadfast can live together. Think of a tree—roots deep, branches wide. Your steady faithfulness in unseen places matters. God keeps the ledger, and nothing done in love is wasted. Even when results hide, heaven sees. Abounding doesn't mean frantic; it means full of life, pouring from a rooted soul. Keep showing up. Your ordinary obedience is building something eternal.

Reflection Question: Where do you need to stay steady and believe your quiet labor matters to God?

Day 82

"For the vision is yet for an appointed time... though it tarry, wait for it; because it will surely come..." — Habakkuk 2:3 (KJV)

God runs on appointment, not accident. Delays are not denials; they're timing. The vision may feel slow, but slow isn't dead. Think of bread rising—nothing seems to happen, yet everything is happening. Rushing can ruin what waiting would perfect. Trust God's calendar. He knows when the doors should open and when your heart is ready to walk through them.

Reflection Question: What promise or vision will you keep trusting God's timing for instead of forcing?

Day 83

"He that believeth on me... out of his belly shall flow rivers of living water." — John 7:38 (KJV)

Renewal doesn't pool; it flows. God fills you so life can spill over—refreshing words, gentle presence, practical help. A stagnant pond grows murky, but a river stays fresh. Keep an open channel: receive from God, release to others. You'll find you're replenished as you pour. Living water isn't scarce. The Source is endlessly generous.

Reflection Question: Where can living water flow from you today to refresh someone weary?

Day 84

"As newborn babes, desire the sincere milk of the word, that ye may grow thereby:" — 1 Peter 2:2 (KJV)

Growth needs nourishment. God's Word is not a chore list; it's food. Babies don't apologize for needing milk—they hunger and grow. Your soul is allowed to be needy for Scripture. Start small, stay consistent, and watch strength quietly build. Over time, you'll crave what once felt hard. That's health. Let the Word do what only it can—feed you into maturity.

Reflection Question: What simple way will you "feed" on Scripture today so your soul can grow?

Day 85

"...that they might be called trees of righteousness, the planting of the LORD, that he might be glorified." — Isaiah 61:3b (KJV)

You are God's planting, not your own PR project. Trees of righteousness don't brag; they bless—shade for the weary, beauty for the broken view, stability in shaky soil. When God plants, He also tends. Your growth tells a story about His goodness. You don't have to force fruit or hurry bloom. Just stay rooted in Him, and let your life quietly point up.

Reflection Question: How can your "shade" bless someone today in a way that points back to God?

Day 86

"The steps of a good man are ordered by the LORD: and he delighteth in his way." — Psalm 37:23 (KJV)

God orders steps, not just leaps. That's comforting when you're unsure which way to go. Take the next right step—the call, the class, the boundary, the rest. As you move, guidance grows. Think of walking with a flashlight at night—you see enough for the next few feet, and that's enough to keep going. God isn't annoyed by your small steps; He delights in them.

Reflection Question: What is your next right step, small but sure, that you sense God ordering?

Day 87

"Forgetting those things which are behind, and reaching forth unto those things which are before..." — *Philippians 3:13 (KJV)*

Forgetting here means loosening your grip, not erasing memory. You can't move forward while clutching old wins or old wounds. Imagine running with a heavy backpack—you'll tire fast. Set it down. Reach forward. God has fresh assignments, new mercies, and grace for the road ahead. The best way to honor your past is to let it inform you, not imprison you.

Reflection Question: What will you release so your hands are free to reach for what's next?

Day 88

"...though our outward man perish, yet the inward man is renewed day by day." — *2 Corinthians 4:16 (KJV)*

Bodies tire. Schedules stretch. But inside, God is doing daily renewal work. Day by day—small refills, quiet strength, fresh perspective. Think of a phone updating overnight—same device, better function. You may not look different, but you're being upgraded within: more resilient, more tender, more anchored. Don't despise the ordinary days; they're the workshop of the inner life.

Reflection Question: Where do you notice God renewing you on the inside, even if life looks the same?

Day 89

"But the path of the just is as the shining light, that shineth more and more unto the perfect day." — Proverbs 4:18 (KJV)

Growth brightens. Not all at once, but "more and more." Like sunrise creeping up your curtains, clarity and courage increase as you walk with God. You may still have shadows, but the light is winning. Keep moving toward what's true, beautiful, and good. By evening, you'll be surprised how far the day's light has reached.

Reflection Question: What small step will move you toward the light so today shines a bit brighter?

Day 90

"Behold, I make all things new." — Revelation 21:5b (KJV)

This is God's heart and His endgame: new. New creation, new order, new joy. Even now, you get previews—reconciled relationships, hearts softened, hope reborn. Every small renewal points to the big one coming. When discouragement whispers, lift your eyes to the promise stamped across eternity: He makes all things new. That includes you, your family, your future. New is not wishful thinking; it's a certainty anchored in the One on the throne.

Reflection Question: How does God's promise to make all things new change how you face today?

Note: March already includes 31 devotionals (Days 60–90). Let's continue with April.

April: Hope and Resurrection

Day 91

"Blessed be the God and Father of our Lord Jesus Christ... hath begotten us again unto a lively hope by the resurrection of Jesus Christ from the dead," — 1 Peter 1:3 (KJV)

Hope is alive because Jesus is. Not wishful thinking—living hope. Like crocuses pushing through stubborn snow, resurrection breaks into cold seasons with color. You may feel stuck in a long winter of waiting or worry. The empty tomb says winter doesn't get the last word. This hope breathes, moves, grows. It doesn't depend on your mood or the headlines; it depends on a risen Savior who keeps His promises. Let this truth warm your day: the same God who raised Jesus is writing new life into your ordinary moments—conversations, commutes, chores. Expect small resurrections: a softened heart, a restored smile, courage returning where fear sat.

Reflection Question: Where do you need to let "lively hope" nudge you to believe for new life today?

Day 92

"Jesus said unto her, I am the resurrection, and the life..." — *John 11:25a (KJV)*

Resurrection isn't just an event; it's a Person. When Martha faced a sealed tomb, Jesus stood in front of her with present-tense hope. We face our own "tombs"—dreams that died, relationships gone cold, plans that fell apart. Jesus meets us there, not with clichés, but with Himself. He can call what's dead to breathe again—or give you life to walk forward without what didn't return. Either way, life is the outcome with Him. If you're staring at a stone today, remember who's beside you. He carries authority over endings and beginnings.

Reflection Question: What sealed place in your life will you invite Jesus, the Resurrection and the Life, to speak into?

Day 93

"But if the Spirit of him that raised up Jesus from the dead dwell in you..." — *Romans 8:11a (KJV)*

Resurrection power isn't just "out there"; it lives in you. Monday-sized strength from an Easter-sized God. The Spirit who woke a dead body to breathing can energize your weary heart, your frayed patience, your discouraged mind. Think of a dead battery boosted by a stronger car—the transfer changes everything. Ask the Spirit to charge what's flat: love for a difficult person, endurance for a hard assignment, hope when circumstances haven't budged. He specializes in reviving what looks done.

Reflection Question: Where do you need the Spirit's resurrection power to recharge you today?

Day 94

"Weeping may endure for a night, but joy cometh in the morning." —
Psalm 30:5b (KJV)

Night feels longer than it is. Tears blur clocks. Yet Scripture promises a sunrise. Joy isn't a denial of grief; it's the light that finds you when grief has done its honest work. Picture pulling back the curtains after a storm—trees still wet, sky washed clean. God doesn't skip your sorrow; He stays through it, then escorts you into new joy. The morning may come slowly—a smile here, a laugh there—but it will come. Hold onto that promise like a warm mug between both hands.

Reflection Question: What small sign of "morning" can you notice and thank God for today?

Day 95

"Which hope we have as an anchor of the soul, both sure and stedfast..."
— Hebrews 6:19a (KJV)

Hope is your anchor, not your balloon. Balloons float with every wind; anchors hold when waves pound. You don't have to feel steady to be steady—you just need something stronger than the storm to hold you. Jesus is that hold. When the news is heavy, when the diagnosis is unclear, when plans shift again, drop your anchor into God's unchanging character. Let Scripture be the chain, prayer the steady rhythm, community the harbor lights that guide you in.

Reflection Question: Where do you need to drop your anchor of hope so your soul can settle?

Day 96

"He is not here: for he is risen, as he said." — Matthew 28:6a (KJV)

The women came expecting a sealed tomb and found an empty one. Hope often surprises us like that—right where we braced for disappointment. "As he said" matters. Jesus keeps His word. When you walk into a situation expecting old outcomes, listen for the angel's reminder: He does what He says. Empty places become starting lines. If God has spoken promise over a weary area of your life, hold space for resurrection. It may not look like you planned, but it will look like He promised.

Reflection Question: What promise has Jesus made that you need to meet with fresh expectancy?

Day 97

"Now the God of hope fill you with all joy and peace in believing... that ye may abound in hope," — Romans 15:13 (KJV)

Hope doesn't trickle; it abounds. God is the Source, and He loves to fill. Joy and peace come as you trust—like air filling a balloon. Believing isn't pretending; it's choosing where to lean. When your mind starts listing what-ifs, turn it toward who He is. Abounding hope spills over onto others. You become the friend who steadies the room, the mom who softens the morning, the coworker who speaks life. That's God's filling at work.

Reflection Question: How will you position your heart to be filled so hope can overflow to someone today?

Day 98

"But now is Christ risen from the dead, and become the firstfruits of them that slept." — 1 Corinthians 15:20 (KJV)

Firstfruits are the first ripe taste that promise a full harvest. Jesus' resurrection is that taste for us. Because He got up, we will too. That future certainty changes today's courage. Think of the first strawberry of the season—small but sweet, telling you more is coming. Let His empty tomb sweeten your waiting, your grieving, your aging. Death doesn't get the finale; Jesus does.

Reflection Question: How does Jesus being "firstfruits" reshape how you face loss or fear today?

Day 99

"For I know that my redeemer liveth..." — Job 19:25a (KJV)

Job said this from a pile of pain, not a beach vacation. Faith can speak life even in ashes. "My Redeemer liveth" means your Rescuer is not retired. He is active, aware, and able. When circumstances shout otherwise, whisper Job's words into your day. Your Redeemer outlives every season that threatens to swallow you. He buys back what's broken and restores what feels ruined—maybe differently than you imagined, but truly.

Reflection Question: Where will you declare, even quietly, "My Redeemer lives," over something hard?

Day 100

"Did not our heart burn within us, while he talked with us by the way...?" — *Luke 24:32 (KJV)*

On the road to Emmaus, disappointment walked beside Jesus and didn't recognize Him at first. Then the Word opened, and hearts warmed. That's how hope often returns—Scripture explained, presence felt, conversation that reorients you. Pay attention to holy heartburn: the warm conviction, the brightening insight, the nudge to turn back toward Jesus. He's closer than you think on your everyday roads.

Reflection Question: When has your heart "burned within" recently, and how will you follow that warmth?

Day 101

"For if we believe that Jesus died and rose again... Wherefore comfort one another with these words." — *1 Thessalonians 4:14, 18 (KJV)*

Resurrection is personal comfort. At gravesides and kitchen tables, we anchor to this: Jesus rose, and so will those who are His. Grief remains real; comfort becomes deeper. We don't comfort with platitudes; we comfort with a Person and a promise. When words feel thin, presence and this hope speak loudest. Death is an enemy, but it's not the end.

Reflection Question: Who needs resurrection-shaped comfort from you, and how can you gently bring it?

Day 102

"...blessed are they that have not seen, and yet have believed." — John 20:29b (KJV)

Thomas needed to see, and Jesus met him graciously. Many days, we won't see first—we'll believe first. That's blessed, Jesus says. Faith often looks like choosing trust before proof: praying before the email arrives, forgiving before the feelings follow, obeying before outcomes are clear. This isn't blind; it's anchored in His character. Believing first opens a doorway for joy to step through.

Reflection Question: What will you choose to believe today even before you see it?

Day 103

"Whom God hath raised up, having loosed the pains of death: because it was not possible that he should be holden of it." — Acts 2:24 (KJV)

Death tried to hold Jesus and couldn't. That impossibility is your hope. Anything that claims final say over you—shame, fear, sin—meets the same power that broke death's grip. Picture handcuffs snapping open. In Christ, what bound you loses authority. You may still feel the echo, but the lock is broken. Walk in that freedom a step at a time; resurrection power meets you in motion.

Reflection Question: What "hold" will you refuse today because Jesus broke its power?

Day 104

"If ye then be risen with Christ, seek those things which are above..." —
Colossians 3:1a (KJV)

Resurrection changes your focus. Raised people look up more. Seeking "things above" isn't ignoring life; it's setting priorities by heaven's light. Think of changing your phone's display from dim to bright—suddenly everything is clearer. With Christ, your values brighten: people over platform, character over image, obedience over convenience. Your feet stay on earth; your gaze rests higher. That's how hope stays fresh.

Reflection Question: What "above" thing will you seek first that could reshape your day on the ground?

Day 105

"Why art thou cast down, O my soul?... hope thou in God: for I shall yet praise him," — *Psalm 42:5 (KJV)*

Talk back to your soul. Not with denial, but with direction. "Yet" is the hinge of hope—praise is coming, even if not today. When your emotions sag like a heavy coat, hang them on a sturdier hook: who God is. The psalmist models honest sadness that still chooses expectation. You can name your low and lift your eyes in the same breath.

Reflection Question: What "yet praise" can you speak over your discouraged places today?

Day 106

"Rejoice not against me, O mine enemy: when I fall, I shall arise..." — *Micah 7:8a (KJV)*

Falling isn't final. Resurrection hope helps you stand up, brush off shame, and learn forward. Maybe you snapped, scrolled too long, or slipped back into an old habit. Don't stay down. In Christ, failure becomes feedback, not your identity. Get up, reach for grace, take the next right step. Your enemy's victory party gets canceled.

Reflection Question: Where do you need to arise—one practical step—after a recent fall?

Day 107

"Arise, shine; for thy light is come, and the glory of the LORD is risen upon thee." — *Isaiah 60:1 (KJV)*

Sunrise language. God's glory has risen over you—so rise into it. This isn't hype; it's holy invitation. Get up in your spirit. Open the blinds on your hope. Maybe it's time to reapply for the job, call the counselor, return to community, begin the habit that makes you whole. Light doesn't demand perfection; it beckons movement. Step into what God is lighting.

Reflection Question: What small "rise and shine" action will you take because God's light is on you?

Day 108

"Who against hope believed in hope..." — Romans 4:18a (KJV)

Abraham believed when evidence was thin. Hope against hope is not stubborn denial; it's steady trust in a Promise-Maker. Maybe the timeline stretched, the odds shrank, and you feel silly still believing. You're in good company. Keep your eyes on the One who calls things that are not as though they were. He writes stories with late plot twists and joyful endings.

Reflection Question: Where do you sense God asking you to believe "against hope" a little longer?

Day 109

"Jesus saith unto them, Come and dine." — John 21:12a (KJV)

After failure and fear, Peter found breakfast on the beach and a Savior who still wanted him. Hope tastes like grilled fish at dawn—ordinary, healing, near. Jesus restores with conversation, not condemnation. He feeds before He fixes. If you feel disqualified, hear His invitation: come and eat. Let grace warm you, then follow again. Second chances are resurrection's everyday gift.

Reflection Question: How will you accept Jesus' invitation to "come and dine" and start again today?

Day 110

"Knowing that he which raised up the Lord Jesus shall raise up us also by Jesus," — 2 Corinthians 4:14a (KJV)

Future resurrection strengthens present resilience. When you know your ending is life, courage grows in the middle. You can live open-handed, love sacrificially, and endure hardship because loss can't have the last word. Death is not your destination; Jesus is. Let that certainty loosen fear's grip and widen your generosity today.

Reflection Question: What courageous choice could you make because your forever is secure in Christ?

Day 111

"This is the day which the LORD hath made; we will rejoice and be glad in it." — Psalm 118:24 (KJV)

Resurrection morning turned an ordinary day into holy celebration. Every day since carries that echo. You don't have to wait for perfect conditions to rejoice; you can choose gladness as an act of faith. Rejoicing doesn't ignore pain; it honors God's presence in it. Find one reason—just one—and let gratitude grow from there. Sometimes joy starts as a whisper and ends as a song.

Reflection Question: What specific reason will you choose to rejoice over in this very day?

Day 112

"I will ransom them from the power of the grave; I will redeem them from death:" — Hosea 13:14a (KJV)

God buys back what the grave tries to steal—hope, purpose, identity. In Christ, the ransom has been paid. You are not owned by despair or defined by what died. Redeemed means reclaimed for use. Think of a thrifted chair restored and set at the table again. God loves to bring you back into the story, useful and beautiful in His hands.

Reflection Question: What part of your life needs to be reclaimed from "grave power" and returned to purpose?

Day 113

"The eyes of your understanding being enlightened; that ye may know what is the hope of his calling," — Ephesians 1:18a (KJV)

Sometimes hope is there—we just need light to see it. Paul prays for brightened eyes. Ask God to turn on the lamp in your understanding so you can spot His calling in your current season. Not a grand stage—your real life: the people you influence, the work you do, the prayers you carry. Hope grows when vision clears.

Reflection Question: Where do you need God to "turn on the light" so you can see hope again?

Day 114

"Because I live, ye shall live also." — John 14:19b (KJV)

Your life is tied to His. Not to your performance, your past, or your predictions—Him. That takes pressure off. Jesus' living becomes your daily permission to live fully: to risk kindness, practice forgiveness, try again. You're not dragging a dead weight of shame; you're carried by a living Lord. Let that union quiet your fear and energize your obedience.

Reflection Question: What will you dare to do today because Jesus lives and your life is in Him?

Day 115

"Who hath abolished death, and hath brought life and immortality to light through the gospel:" — 2 Timothy 1:10b (KJV)

Jesus didn't just survive death; He abolished its rule. He turned on the lights in a room we all feared. Immortality isn't a fairy tale; it's your future in Him. When the temporary feels total, remember the bigger story. You can hold today loosely and love deeply because the end is secure and stunningly good. Let eternity steady your choices and sweeten your attitude.

Reflection Question: How does Jesus abolishing death change the way you face today's temporary pressures?

Day 116

"We are buried with him by baptism into death... even so we also should walk in newness of life." — Romans 6:4 (KJV)

Resurrection life isn't just a future event; it's a present walk. Newness looks like fresh patterns in familiar places—choosing truth over spin, gentleness over heat, faith over fret. Baptism is the picture: the old goes under, the new comes up. You can leave yesterday's scripts in the water and take a new step today. Walk it out in sneakers and schedules, one choice at a time.

Reflection Question: What "newness of life" step will you take in a very practical area today?

Day 117

"My flesh and my heart faileth: but God is the strength of my heart, and my portion for ever." — Psalm 73:26 (KJV)

Bodies tire. Plans fail. But God remains. He doesn't just give strength; He is your strength. When limits show up, let them usher you to His enoughness. Portion means He is the part that satisfies when other parts are missing. Hope grows when you trade self-sufficiency for God-dependency. Weakness becomes a doorway, not a dead end.

Reflection Question: Where will you lean into God as your strength and portion instead of pushing harder?

Day 118

"For the Lord will not cast off for ever: But though he cause grief, yet will he have compassion according to the multitude of his mercies." —
Lamentations 3:31-32 (KJV)

Grief is not God's final word. Compassion is. Even in discipline or hard providence, His mercies are many and near. If you feel sidelined or unsure how to come back, hear this: He does not discard His daughters. His compassion outnumbers your failures and outweighs your fears. Let mercy lead you home to hope.

Reflection Question: How can you receive God's compassion today and let it ease your grief?

Day 119

"But go your way, tell his disciples and Peter that he goeth before you into Galilee:" — Mark 16:7a (KJV)

"And Peter." Two words of tender hope to the man who had denied Him. Jesus goes ahead, and He includes the one who blew it. If you've disqualified yourself, hear your name in that sentence. He still calls you back to where it all began—Galilee places of simple obedience and fresh love. He goes before you, preparing the next step.

Reflection Question: Where is your "Galilee," and what step will you take toward Jesus who goes before you?

Day 120

"And God shall wipe away all tears from their eyes... there shall be no more death, neither sorrow, nor crying..." — *Revelation 21:4a (KJV)*

This is where hope is headed: tearless, deathless, healed. God Himself will wipe your tears—not outsource it—personal, gentle, final. Knowing the end brightens the middle. You can face hard news with soft courage, mourn with hope, and invest in what lasts. Every small resurrection now points to the great one coming. Lift your chin. The best is not behind you in Christ; it's before you.

Reflection Question: How does this promised future shape one choice you'll make before the day ends?

MAY: GRATITUDE AND JOY

Day 121

"O give thanks unto the LORD; for he is good: because his mercy endureth for ever." — Psalm 118:1 (KJV)

Gratitude starts small and grows strong. It's noticing hot coffee, a beam of morning sun on the counter, a text that lands at the right time. Thankfulness doesn't wait for perfect days; it makes ordinary days brighter. God's goodness isn't moody. His mercy doesn't run out like battery life. When you say, "Thank You," you're not ignoring hard things—you're opening windows so light can get in. Gratitude rewires your perspective, like switching a room from fluorescent to warm light. Try naming God's goodness in the now. Watch how your shoulders drop and your heart softens. Mercy that lasts forever can handle today.

Reflection Question: What simple good can you thank God for in this very moment?

Day 122

"Rejoice evermore. Pray without ceasing. In every thing give thanks..."
— 1 Thessalonians 5:16-18 (KJV)

This is a rhythm more than a rule: rejoice, pray, give thanks. It's like breathing for your soul—in, out, repeat. Rejoice when good news hits. Pray when you're unsure. Give thanks while you wait. Not for everything, but in everything. Gratitude doesn't need a bow on the package to begin; it trusts the Giver even when the wrapping's messy. Think of a day set to music— these three beats keep you from slipping into silence or noise. Joy is the melody, prayer the harmony, thanks the drum keeping time.

Reflection Question: Which beat—rejoice, pray, or give thanks— needs turning up in your day?

Day 123

"Rejoice in the Lord alway: and again I say, Rejoice." — Philippians 4:4
(KJV)

Paul repeats himself because we forget. Rejoice in the Lord— not in results, likes, or weather. Joy that anchors in Him holds during delays and disappointments. Think of a buoy in choppy water—it bobs but doesn't sink. Rejoicing is choosing where your gladness lives. It can be as simple as humming a worship song while folding towels, or smiling because God is still who He said He is. Joy becomes a holy habit that changes the room when you walk in.

Reflection Question: How will you rejoice in the Lord—specifically, not generally—today?

Day 124

"Enter into his gates with thanksgiving, and into his courts with praise..." — *Psalm 100:4 (KJV)*

Thanksgiving is the key that opens the front door to God's presence. You don't have to arrive polished. Just come with thanks. Picture stepping into a warm house after a cold day—gratitude is that first breath of heat. Praise follows naturally when you realize whose house you're in: the One who knows you, loves you, and welcomes you home. Start your prayers with "Thank You," and watch how your worries take their proper size.

Reflection Question: What thank-you will you bring first when you step into prayer?

Day 125

"Every good gift and every perfect gift is from above..." — *James 1:17 (KJV)*

Gifts are everywhere when you look up. A friend who checks in. A meal that hits just right. Strength to keep going. These aren't random; they're delivered from a steady Giver who doesn't change with the seasons. Gratitude connects the dots—this came from God. It turns common into sacred: Tuesday traffic becomes prayer time; a garden bloom becomes a love note. Naming gifts trains your heart to trust the Giver for tomorrow's needs too.

Reflection Question: What "ordinary gift" will you trace back to God and thank Him for?

Day 126

"...for the joy of the LORD is your strength." — Nehemiah 8:10 (KJV)

Joy isn't just a feeling; it's fuel. God's joy—His delight in you and His unchanging goodness—strengthens shaky knees. On days you're tired of being strong, let His joy carry some weight. Think of a friend who shows up with dinner; suddenly the evening feels doable. God's joy does that for your soul. It doesn't demand a grin; it supplies grit with a smile somewhere in it.

Reflection Question: Where do you need to lean on God's joy as your strength today?

Day 127

"Thou wilt shew me the path of life: in thy presence is fulness of joy..."
— Psalm 16:11 (KJV)

Fullness of joy isn't in a perfect plan; it's in a present God. Joy expands when you stay close. Think of walking a trail with a guide—you relax because you're with someone who knows the way. God's presence makes the path less about pressure and more about companionship. The future may still be fuzzy, but your feet are steady. Joy isn't a destination; it's the company you keep as you go.

Reflection Question: How can you practice God's presence so joy can fill the space you're in?

Day 128

"And let the peace of God rule in your hearts... and be ye thankful." —
Colossians 3:15 (KJV)

Let peace call the shots, and let gratitude be the tone. When emotions flare, thanksgiving cools the room. Peace rules when you choose thankfulness over nitpicking, remembering what's right before rehearsing what's wrong. Picture an umpire making the call—gratitude often decides close plays in relationships. "Thank you" softens edges, including your own.

Reflection Question: Where could a sincere "thank you" help peace rule in your heart or home?

Day 129

"Bless the LORD, O my soul, and forget not all his benefits:" — *Psalm 103:2 (KJV)*

Forgetfulness steals joy. David tells his soul to remember: forgiveness, healing, mercy, rescue. Make a mental highlight reel—times God came through, big and small. When anxiety rewinds worst-case scenarios, let gratitude play the truth back. Memory becomes worship. Your story tells you something important: God has been faithful. That isn't just history; it's hope with receipts.

Reflection Question: Which benefit of God do you most need to remember and bless Him for today?

Day 130

"By him therefore let us offer the sacrifice of praise to God continually..." — *Hebrews 13:15 (KJV)*

Some praise feels costly. You sing while waiting, thank Him while hurting, bless Him through tears. That's a sacrifice—and it's beautiful to God. He doesn't ask for fake smiles. He invites honest worship that says, "You're worthy, even now." Think of a candle lit in a power outage—it matters more because it's dark. Your praise in the dark pushes back the night.

Reflection Question: What hard place needs the candlelight of your honest praise today?

Day 131

"And one of them... turned back, and with a loud voice glorified God... giving him thanks:" — *Luke 17:15-16 (KJV)*

Ten were healed; one returned. Gratitude turns back. It doesn't rush past the Giver on the way to the next thing. The Samaritan fell at Jesus' feet—no cool composure, just loud thanks. Sometimes joy is noisy. What has God done that deserves a return trip? Circle back. Say it out loud. Gratitude deepens the gift and multiplies the joy.

Reflection Question: What answered prayer or kindness will you "turn back" and thank Jesus for today?

Day 132

"Thou hast turned for me my mourning into dancing... O LORD my God, I will give thanks unto thee for ever." — Psalm 30:11-12 (KJV)

God is a changer of seasons. He doesn't hurry grief, but He can shift it into joy in time. Think of winter thawing—ice loosens, water runs, birds return. Maybe you're not twirling yet; maybe you're just tapping your toe again. That's a start. Thank Him for any sign of movement. Gratitude keeps your heart limber so when the music swells, you're ready to dance.

Reflection Question: What tiny "toe tap" of joy can you thank God for in this season?

Day 133

"These things have I spoken unto you, that my joy might remain in you, and that your joy might be full." — John 15:11 (KJV)

Jesus wants you full—not of stress, but of His joy. Remain means it stays, not just pops in on holidays. Full joy doesn't mean every problem is solved; it means you're held. Think of a thermos that keeps warmth in the cold—His words do that for your soul. Stay near what He's said, and your joy retains heat, even outside in the chill.

Reflection Question: Which words of Jesus will you keep close so joy can stay warm today?

Day 134

"It is a good thing to give thanks unto the LORD, and to sing praises unto thy name, O most High:" — Psalm 92:1 (KJV)

Some things are always good—like saying "thank You" to God. Singing lifts the ceiling of your heart. You don't have to be on pitch to tune your soul. Put praise in your mouth and see how your mood follows. Gratitude is good for you and pleasing to Him—a two-way blessing.

Reflection Question: What song of thanks can you whisper or blast to lift your heart today?

Day 135

"Thanks be unto God for his unspeakable gift." — 2 Corinthians 9:15 (KJV)

Some gifts defy adjectives. Jesus is that gift—grace you can't measure, love you can't exhaust. When words run out, gratitude still has a way of bowing the heart. Let "thank You for Jesus" be the baseline of your day. Other blessings fit under that big umbrella, safe and steady. Unspeakable doesn't mean unspoken; it means the more you speak, the more wonder you find.

Reflection Question: How can you center your gratitude on Jesus, the Gift beyond words?

Day 136

"Then was our mouth filled with laughter... The LORD hath done great things for us; whereof we are glad." — Psalm 126:2-3 (KJV)

Holy laughter is a thing. When God restores, smiles return. Maybe slowly, maybe suddenly—but they do. Think of a long-awaited call finally coming, or a door that wouldn't budge swinging open. Gladness is not shallow; it's a deep exhale when you remember who brought you here. Share the story. Laughter shared doubles joy and gives others hope for their turn.

Reflection Question: What "great thing" has God done that you can gladly celebrate today?

Day 137

"Therefore with joy shall ye draw water out of the wells of salvation." — Isaiah 12:3 (KJV)

Salvation isn't a dry well; it's a deep one. Joy draws water. When you feel parched, lower the bucket—remember you're forgiven, loved, and kept. Pull up enough for you and a cup for a friend. The well doesn't run out. Sometimes you have to choose to draw when feelings are thin. Joy comes as you haul grace into your day, one bucket at a time.

Reflection Question: What truth of your salvation will you draw up to refresh your heart today?

Day 138

"A merry heart doeth good like a medicine: but a broken spirit drieth the bones." — *Proverbs 17:22 (KJV)*

God isn't against your laughter. He prescribes it. Joy doesn't ignore pain; it brings relief, like a good dose of kindness and humor on a hard day. Let yourself enjoy what's good—fresh strawberries, a silly meme, a sunset that refuses to be ordinary. A merry heart heals in ways you can't chart on a spreadsheet. It's a gift to you and to those near you.

Reflection Question: What simple joy can you let yourself enjoy as good medicine today?

Day 139

"Rejoicing in hope; patient in tribulation; continuing instant in prayer;" — *Romans 12:12 (KJV)*

Three moves for tough days: rejoice in hope (lift your eyes), be patient in trouble (slow your breathing), stay quick in prayer (keep talking to God). Joy and patience grow stronger together. Prayer ties them off so they don't unravel. You don't have to be impressive; you can be steady. That's beautiful strength.

Reflection Question: Which of these three moves do you need most right now—and how will you practice it?

Day 140

"...my cup runneth over." — Psalm 23:5 (KJV)

Overflow isn't always extra stuff; it's extra awareness. God keeps pouring—comfort in grief, guidance in confusion, kindness in small surprises. Sometimes your cup runs over into someone else's. That's the point. You're blessed to be a blessing. Notice the overflow and look for where it's spilling—maybe into a neighbor's need or a child's day.

Reflection Question: Where is your cup running over, and who might God be nudging you to share with?

Day 141

"O give thanks unto the LORD; for he is good; for his mercy endureth for ever." — 1 Chronicles 16:34 (KJV)

We circle back to this because it's bedrock: God is good. His mercy lasts. When the week is a blur, let this be the sentence you can still say. Gratitude anchored here steadies you when outcomes wobble. You're not clinging to a mood; you're leaning on a Person whose character doesn't shift with your calendar.

Reflection Question: How will you anchor your thanks to God's goodness when plans change?

Day 142

"Let us come before his presence with thanksgiving, and make a joyful noise unto him with psalms." — Psalm 95:2 (KJV)

You're invited to bring noise and thanks. You don't need a choir robe—just a willing heart. Joyful noise might be a whispered hymn in the car, a shout in the kitchen, or a hum while you walk. God isn't grading pitch; He's welcoming presence. Thanksgiving turns your approach into celebration, not obligation.

Reflection Question: What joyful noise will you bring to God's presence today?

Day 143

"...your heart shall rejoice, and your joy no man taketh from you." — John 16:22 (KJV)

Jesus promises a kind of joy that can't be stolen. Not by critics, not by circumstances, not by delays. That joy lives deeper than mood. It comes from being His. When something tries to swipe your gladness, picture locking your heart's joy in a safe with this promise on the door. You can grieve and still be held by a joy that stays.

Reflection Question: What tries to steal your joy, and how will you guard it with Jesus' promise?

Day 144

"For all things are for your sakes, that the abundant grace might through the thanksgiving of many redound to the glory of God." — 2 Corinthians 4:15 (KJV)

Grace grows louder through shared thanks. When we tell our stories and give God credit, His glory echoes wider. Your gratitude might be the match that lights someone else's hope. Think of a stadium wave—one person starts, and soon the whole place is moving. Thanksgiving spreads like that. Small testimonies become big praise.

Reflection Question: Who can you tell—simply—what God has done so shared thanks can grow?

Day 145

"I thank my God upon every remembrance of you," — Philippians 1:3 (KJV)

People are gifts, not projects. Paul's first instinct when he thought of friends was gratitude. Who brings color to your days? A mentor, a neighbor, a sibling? Thank God for them, and if you can, tell them. Gratitude strengthens bonds and nudges comparisons out the door. Relationships thrive where thanks is spoken often.

Reflection Question: Who came to mind just now, and how will you express thanks for them?

Day 146

"And whatsoever ye do... do all in the name of the Lord Jesus, giving thanks to God and the Father by him." — Colossians 3:17 (KJV)

Whatever is wide. Dishes, deadlines, diapers, decisions—do them with Jesus in view and thanks in your mouth. Gratitude turns chores into worship and meetings into ministry. It lifts your eyes from "I have to" to "I get to, with Him." If you can't do it with thanks, it might need a new approach—or a no.

Reflection Question: What ordinary task can you reframe as worship by doing it with thanks?

Day 147

"Thou crownest the year with thy goodness; and thy paths drop fatness."
— Psalm 65:11 (KJV)

God's goodness rings your year like a crown. Even in lean months, His path leaves abundance—provision you didn't expect, favor you couldn't plan. Look back and you'll spot generous crumbs: open doors, timely help, a peace that made no sense. Gratitude ties the months together with a golden thread.

Reflection Question: What trail of God's goodness can you see behind you that deserves thanks?

Day 148

"As ye have therefore received Christ Jesus the Lord, so walk ye in him... abounding therein with thanksgiving." — Colossians 2:6-7 (KJV)

You started by grace; keep walking that way—with thanks that keeps overflowing. Rooted people abound in gratitude because they know Who holds them. When life shakes, roots grip soil, and the heart says, "Thank You for holding me." Abounding thanks isn't forced; it's the natural response of a life built on Jesus.

Reflection Question: How can you take one "grace step" today and let thanksgiving abound as you do?

Day 149

"...ye rejoice with joy unspeakable and full of glory:" — 1 Peter 1:8 (KJV)

Joy unspeakable sounds dramatic, but it shows up in quiet kitchens too. It's the glow that comes from believing Jesus loves you without seeing Him yet. Some days, words won't capture it—you'll just know your heart feels lighter. Glory doesn't wait for heaven to start; it leaks into earth through trusting hearts. Let yourself enjoy that gift when it comes.

Reflection Question: Where have you tasted "joy unspeakable," and how can you lean toward it today?

Day 150

"For the LORD taketh pleasure in his people: he will beautify the meek with salvation." — Psalm 149:4 (KJV)

God delights in you. Sit with that. His pleasure isn't based on your perfect performance but on His perfect love. Salvation beautifies—humble hearts glow with a joy you can't buy. When you know you're delighted in, you stop striving to be dazzling. Gratitude rises naturally: "Thank You for loving me, as me." Joy follows close behind.

Reflection Question: How does knowing God takes pleasure in you change your posture today?

Day 151

"Giving thanks always for all things unto God and the Father in the name of our Lord Jesus Christ;" — Ephesians 5:20 (KJV)

Always and all things feel big. But this is about a direction, not perfection. As you move through your day, tilt your heart toward thanks. For the meal and for the lesson in the hard conversation. For the green lights and the delays that protected you from what you'll never know. In Jesus' name ties your thanks to the One who makes every gift possible. Gratitude becomes the soundtrack of a life that knows it's held.

Reflection Question: What's one "always and all things" moment you can thank God for before you sleep?

June: Strength in Weakness

Day 152

"My grace is sufficient for thee: for my strength is made perfect in weakness." — 2 Corinthians 12:9 (KJV)

Weakness is where grace does its best work. You don't have to pretend you're fine or power through every task. Think of a cracked cup held under a faucet—the water still pours, and somehow the cracks make you notice the source more. God's strength fills the places that feel thin: the hard conversation, the endless caregiving, the worry that wakes you at 3 a.m. Instead of hiding the cracks, bring them to Him. His power isn't an add-on after you've tried everything; it's the starting place. He's not disappointed you need Him—He delights to meet you.

Reflection Question: Where will you bring your weakness to Jesus so His strength can shine through?

Day 153

"He giveth power to the faint; and to them that have no might he increaseth strength." — Isaiah 40:29 (KJV)

Some days, "no might" feels like your address. The sink is full, the inbox overflows, and your patience is thin. God meets you there. He doesn't scold you for being tired; He supplies what you lack. Picture a phone on 1% sliding onto the charger—the power is borrowed, but it's real. His strength doesn't make you superhuman; it makes you sustained. When you've reached your end, you're right at His beginning. Breathe. Ask. Receive. Strength grows in the asking.

Reflection Question: Where do you feel faint today, and how will you ask God to increase your strength?

Day 154

"God is our refuge and strength, a very present help in trouble." — Psalm 46:1 (KJV)

Refuge means there's a place to run. Not someday—now. God is "very present," not distant or distracted. When trouble knocks—health scares, financial strain, family tension—don't just pace the hallway; step into the shelter. Imagine a storm shelter door swinging open; inside, the wind is still loud, but it can't touch you. That's what His presence is like. Strength isn't the absence of storms; it's safety within them. Let your first instinct be to run toward Him, not away.

Reflection Question: What trouble could you carry into God's refuge instead of carrying alone?

Day 155

"I can do all things through Christ which strengtheneth me." —
Philippians 4:13 (KJV)

"All things" doesn't mean everything on everyone's list. It means everything Christ gives you to do today—with His strength, not your strain. You can make the call. You can set the boundary. You can get through the appointment. Think of a teammate handing you the right tool for the job—Jesus equips you for what He asks. This verse isn't about hustle; it's about Help. When you hit your limit, remember whose strength you're using.

Reflection Question: What specific "today thing" will you face leaning on Christ's strength, not your own?

Day 156

"In returning and rest shall ye be saved; in quietness and in confidence
shall be your strength:" — Isaiah 30:15a (KJV)

Strength sometimes looks like stillness. Returning to God, resting in His care, quieting the urge to fix everything—this is power in a noisy world. Imagine turning down the car radio to hear directions you were missing. Quietness isn't passivity; it's clarity. Confidence grows when you remember who sits on the throne and who holds your hand. You don't have to match the world's speed to live strong. Slow can be spiritual.

Reflection Question: Where can you practice quiet trust today and let strength rise in the calm?

Day 157

"The LORD is the strength of my life; of whom shall I be afraid?" —
Psalm 27:1b (KJV)

Fear shrinks when you remember your Source. If strength came from your résumé or your bank account, worry would be reasonable. But your strength is a Person. He lights your path and guards your steps. Picture a porch light that flips on the moment you open the door; fear loses its mystery in the light. Walk forward with the One who makes courage possible, not because you're fearless, but because you're accompanied.

Reflection Question: How does remembering God as your strength change what you fear today?

Day 158

"After that ye have suffered a while, make you perfect, stablish, strengthen, settle you." — *1 Peter 5:10b (KJV)*

Suffering feels endless, but Scripture says "a while." God doesn't waste it; He uses it to establish and steady you. Like a tree that's weathered wind, your roots grip deeper. Being "settled" doesn't remove the memory of pain; it adds a new stability: you've seen God hold you. Strength here is quiet and mature—the kind that listens more, rushes less, and trusts sooner. Your story is being shaped by a faithful God who finishes what He starts.

Reflection Question: Where can you notice the settling work God has grown in you through hard seasons?

Day 159

"Be strong in the Lord, and in the power of his might." — Ephesians 6:10 (KJV)

"Be strong" can feel like pressure until you hear the rest: in the Lord. Not in caffeine, not in resolve, in Him. Think about plugging a lamp into the wall—light happens not because the lamp tries hard, but because it's connected. Your strength comes from His power. Stay close. Pray often. Put truth in your ears. Then stand. Strength isn't always loud; sometimes it's simply not quitting.

Reflection Question: What helps you stay connected to God's power so you can stand today?

Day 160

"God hath chosen the weak things of the world to confound the things which are mighty;" — 1 Corinthians 1:27b (KJV)

God loves using unlikely people. Your lack is not a liability in His hands; it's a platform for His power. A simple lunch fed a crowd. A shepherd's sling dropped a giant. A hesitant voice shared hope with a friend. Weakness keeps you humble and close. That's the sweet spot where God gets the credit and you get the joy of watching Him work through everyday you.

Reflection Question: What small, weak thing can you offer God and trust Him to use?

Day 161

"For I the LORD thy God will hold thy right hand, saying unto thee, Fear not; I will help thee." — Isaiah 41:13 (KJV)

Held hands change everything. A held hand steadies a toddler crossing the street and calms a patient before surgery. God says He holds yours. This isn't a pep talk; it's a promise of presence and help. You may still walk through the appointment, the meeting, the conversation—but you won't walk alone. Listen for His whisper: Fear not. I will help. Then take the next step with that Hand in yours.

Reflection Question: What step will you take today trusting the God who holds your hand?

Day 162

"In the day when I cried thou answeredst me, and strengthenedst me with strength in my soul." — Psalm 138:3 (KJV)

Some strength shows up inside before anything changes outside. You pray—maybe messy, maybe short—and something settles. Soul-strength is that quiet courage that helps you walk back into the same room with new peace. It's not adrenaline; it's assurance. God answers not only by fixing situations but by fortifying hearts. Keep calling. He hears. He strengthens in ways you can feel.

Reflection Question: Where do you need "strength in your soul," and will you ask God for it today?

Day 163

"Thou therefore, my son, be strong in the grace that is in Christ Jesus."
— 2 Timothy 2:1 (KJV)

Grace is not just pardon; it's power. "Be strong in grace" means lean into what Jesus gives, not what you can earn. When you mess up, grace helps you get up. When you're tempted to prove yourself, grace reminds you you're already loved. That takes the pressure off and puts strength on. It's like switching from carrying your groceries to rolling them in a cart—same load, new ease.

Reflection Question: Where do you need to trade self-effort for grace-powered strength today?

Day 164

"But the Lord is faithful, who shall stablish you, and keep you from evil." — 2 Thessalonians 3:3 (KJV)

Your stability doesn't rest on your willpower; it rests on a faithful Lord. He establishes you—sets your feet on solid ground—and protects you from harm you see and harm you don't. Think of a security system you didn't install, quietly guarding your home. God's faithfulness is like that: steady, often unseen, always active. Let His keeping calm your anxious what-ifs.

Reflection Question: How does God's faithfulness help you stand steadier in a shaky area today?

Day 165

"Be strong and of a good courage... for the LORD thy God, he it is that doth go with thee; he will not fail thee," — Deuteronomy 31:6a, c (KJV)

Courage grows when you know who's going with you. God doesn't send you into hard places with a thumbs-up; He accompanies you. He won't fail or bail. Picture a friend who never flakes—multiplied by infinity. Strength here looks like steady steps: make the call, show up, try again. Not because you feel brave, but because you're not alone.

Reflection Question: Where do you need to take a courageous step because God goes with you?

Day 166

"Be strong and of a good courage... for the LORD thy God is with thee whithersoever thou goest." — Joshua 1:9b (KJV)

"Wherever" includes the office, the carpool, the hospital, the quiet house. God's with-ness turns ordinary places into holy ground. Strength is location-proof because His presence travels. When dread tries to narrate your day, interrupt it with this: He's here, and He's not leaving. Courage is often a whisper, not a roar—but it's real.

Reflection Question: What place today becomes braver because you remember God is with you there?

Day 167

"Strengthen ye the weak hands, and confirm the feeble knees. Say to them that are of a fearful heart, Be strong, fear not:" — Isaiah 35:3-4a (KJV)

We're not meant to muscle through alone. God calls us to strengthen each other—steady hands that shake, knees that want to buckle. Sometimes strength is a text at the right time, a meal on a hard day, or simply, "I'm with you." Your encouragement can be borrowed strength for someone's fearful heart. That's holy work. As you lift others, you'll find your own courage rising too.

Reflection Question: Who needs borrowed strength from you today, and what simple encouragement can you give?

Day 168

"Blessed is the man whose strength is in thee... They go from strength to strength," — Psalm 84:5, 7a (KJV)

Strength in God multiplies, not drains. You start with little, and somehow there's more by day's end. It's like walking from one shaded rest stop to the next on a hot trail—enough for this stretch, then enough again. Blessed means deeply happy, well-supplied. Put your weight on Him, and watch how He carries you from one grace to another, one strength to the next.

Reflection Question: Where have you seen God move you "from strength to strength" lately?

Day 169

"...but David encouraged himself in the LORD his God." — 1 Samuel 30:6b (KJV)

Sometimes the room is empty and you have to preach hope to your own heart. David did. He reached for God when everything felt lost. Encouraging yourself isn't pretending; it's reminding. You replay truth: God is good, God is here, God will help. You sing a song. You recall an old rescue. You choose to believe before you feel it. That small turn toward God can shift the whole day.

Reflection Question: What truth will you speak to your own heart to find courage in God today?

Day 170

"Strengthened with all might, according to his glorious power, unto all patience and longsuffering with joyfulness;" — Colossians 1:11 (KJV)

God strengthens you not just for big battles, but for long waits. Patience and endurance with joy—that's supernatural. Anyone can wait while grumbling; grace helps you wait with a soft spirit. Think of cruise control on a long highway—keeps you steady without constant strain. God's power sets the pace so you don't burn out. Joy doesn't remove the wait; it lightens it.

Reflection Question: Where do you need God's strength for patient endurance with a joyful spirit?

Day 171

"Strength and honour are her clothing; and she shall rejoice in time to come." — Proverbs 31:25 (KJV)

God dresses His daughters in strength, not stress. This isn't about a perfect schedule; it's about a settled heart. Honour means dignity—how you carry yourself when life is loud. Joy "in time to come" hints at a hopeful future. Wear what God gives: courage stitched with kindness, steadiness lined with grace. It looks good on you.

Reflection Question: What does it look like for you to "put on" strength and dignity in a practical way today?

Day 172

"We have this treasure in earthen vessels, that the excellency of the power may be of God, and not of us." — 2 Corinthians 4:7 (KJV)

Clay jars chip. That's us—fragile, ordinary. Yet God places His treasure within. The point isn't to hide the chips; it's to let the light through them. When you love in your tiredness, forgive in your weakness, or show up when you feel small, people see a power that isn't yours. That's the beauty of being a vessel: you carry what's priceless, even if you feel plain.

Reflection Question: How might your "earthen" limits help God's power shine through today?

Day 173

"And the LORD shall guide thee continually... and make fat thy bones: and thou shalt be like a watered garden," — *Isaiah 58:11 (KJV)*

Continual guidance and strengthened bones—God cares for your path and your stamina. A "watered garden" doesn't hustle; it receives. Then it flourishes—green, steady, fruitful. Let God's voice lead your decisions, big and small. Let His care replenish what life drains. The result isn't just surviving; it's quiet thriving, even in dry places.

Reflection Question: Where do you need God's ongoing guidance so your strength can be replenished?

Day 174

"If thou faint in the day of adversity, thy strength is small." — *Proverbs 24:10 (KJV)*

This verse isn't a shame stamp; it's a check-engine light. If adversity knocks you flat, you may be running on your own fuel. Let it drive you to the Station. Small strength can become great when the source changes. Ask, "Whose power am I using?" God invites you to trade panic for dependence, hurry for help. The test reveals, then redirects.

Reflection Question: What adversity is revealing small strength—and how will you shift to God's supply?

Day 175

"Watch ye and pray, lest ye enter into temptation. The spirit truly is ready, but the flesh is weak." — Mark 14:38 (KJV)

Good intentions aren't enough. The gap between "I want to" and "I did" is where prayer fits. Watching means staying alert to your patterns—late-night scrolling, snappy replies, old coping. Prayer invites power into that gap. Weak flesh isn't an excuse; it's a reminder to reach for help. Stay awake to your heart and talk to God in the moment, not just after the moment.

Reflection Question: Where do you need to "watch and pray" so your weak spots don't lead you astray?

Day 176

"The LORD is my strength and song, and is become my salvation." — Psalm 118:14 (KJV)

Strength and song belong together. God doesn't just help you lift the load; He puts music in your mouth while you carry it. Salvation changes the soundtrack—from fear to praise. Maybe today the song is quiet—a hum while you wash dishes or a lyric that steadies your commute. That's still holy. Sing because He saves and sustains.

Reflection Question: What "song" (even a line) can you carry today as a reminder of God's strength?

Day 177

"The LORD God is my strength, and he will make my feet like hinds' feet," — Habakkuk 3:19a (KJV)

Mountain goats don't need flat ground; they have steady feet for steep places. God gives that kind of footing. Your terrain may be rough—new diagnosis, tight finances, complex decisions—yet you can move with surprising stability. He doesn't always flatten the hill; He fits your feet for it. One careful step at a time, you'll find yourself standing where you didn't think you could.

Reflection Question: What steep place are you climbing, and how can you take one sure step with God?

Day 178

"Let us therefore come boldly unto the throne of grace... and find grace to help in time of need." — Hebrews 4:16 (KJV)

Boldly doesn't mean arrogantly; it means confidently, like a child who knows she's welcome. God's throne is not a courtroom for your condemnation; it's a help desk for your need. Come as you are—flustered, unsure, in a hurry—and ask for specific help. Grace meets you with what fits: wisdom, patience, courage, calm. There's no quota on requests. The door stays open.

Reflection Question: What time-of-need will you bring boldly to God's throne for help today?

Day 179

"Cast thy burden upon the LORD, and he shall sustain thee:" — Psalm 55:22a (KJV)

Burdens are meant to be thrown, not cradled. Casting looks messy—short prayers, sighs, tears. God can handle all of it. Sustain means He doesn't just take the weight; He carries you through. Picture shifting a heavy backpack onto stronger shoulders—you still walk, but without the ache. Offload what's too heavy. His hands are big enough.

Reflection Question: What specific burden will you toss onto God instead of shouldering alone?

Day 180

"Now unto him that is able to keep you from falling," — Jude 24a (KJV)

You're not kept by your grip on God, but by His grip on you. He's able to keep you—through temptation, discouragement, complexity. Think of walking with someone steady on an icy path; their hold makes all the difference. Your steps may slip, but the keeping is sure. Relax the fear of failure and rest in the One who holds.

Reflection Question: Where does God's keeping power let you trade fear for confidence today?

Day 181

"Arise and eat; because the journey is too great for thee." — *1 Kings 19:7b (KJV)*

Elijah was exhausted and done. God didn't preach at him; He fed him. Sometimes the most spiritual thing is a nap and a meal offered by grace. "Too great for thee" is not failure language; it's invitation language—to receive strength you don't have. Let God care for your body and soul. Eat what He provides: Scripture, rest, encouragement, practical help. Then get up and go on, not by hustle, but by His kindness.

Reflection Question: What simple provision from God—rest, food, Scripture, help—do you need to receive so you can continue?

July: Courage, Calling, and Sisterhood

Day 182

"Fear not: for I have redeemed thee, I have called thee by thy name; thou art mine." — Isaiah 43:1 (KJV)

There's a name tag on your heart, and God wrote it. Not "Not enough." Not "Too much." Your true label is "Mine." On mornings you feel invisible—lost in laundry, meetings, or expectations—this verse pulls you into focus. Redeemed means bought back, wanted, chosen. God knows your story and still calls you by name, not by your past or your pressure. Like hearing your name across a crowded room, it makes you lift your head. You're not trying to earn place or prove worth. You already belong. That shifts how you enter rooms, answer texts, and make choices. Loved women walk lighter.

Reflection Question: Where will you walk differently today because you remember, "I am His"?

Day 183

"Stand fast therefore in the liberty wherewith Christ hath made us free," — Galatians 5:1a (KJV)

Freedom isn't just fireworks and flags—it's everyday choices unchained by old fears. In Christ, you're free from the pressure to perform, the comparison scroll, the guilt that keeps circling. Freedom looks like a clean inbox in your soul. Stand fast means hold your ground when old habits tug. When the "shoulds" get loud, answer with grace. Jesus didn't set you free so you'd tiptoe back to prison. He unlocked the door and said, "Walk with Me." That's a summer breeze through a stuffy room.

Reflection Question: What familiar chain will you refuse today because Christ set you free?

Day 184

"She openeth her mouth with wisdom; and in her tongue is the law of kindness." — Proverbs 31:26 (KJV)

Wise words don't have to be long; they just have to be kind. You know the power of tone—how a gentle reply can land soft after a hard day. Wisdom listens before speaking. Kindness chooses words that heal, not score points. Picture your tongue like a thermostat; it sets the temperature in the room. You can calm a tense meeting, settle a child, and steady your own heart with the way you speak. That's not natural; that's Spirit-helped strength wrapped in gentleness.

Reflection Question: Which conversation today needs fewer words and more kindness from you?

Day 185

"Come ye yourselves apart into a desert place, and rest a while:" — *Mark 6:31a (KJV)*

Even Jesus told tired friends to rest. Not because the needs vanished, but because people do. Rest isn't laziness; it's trust—laying down the cape because you remember you're not the Savior. "Apart" might be a quiet porch, a slow walk, a screen break, a nap without guilt. Rest lets your soul catch up to your schedule. The to-do list may still be long, but your heart breathes. From that place, you offer better love, better work, better you.

Reflection Question: Where can you step "apart" for a small, guilt-free rest so your soul can breathe?

Day 186

"I will praise thee; for I am fearfully and wonderfully made:" — *Psalm 139:14a (KJV)*

Your mirror tells one story; God tells another. He calls you wonderfully made—on purpose, with care. That includes your laugh, your curly hair or straight, your freckles, your strengths, even the parts you're learning to love. When body talk gets loud, anchor to this: God didn't make a mistake with you. Treat yourself like someone God loves—sleep, move, eat, speak kindly. Gratitude for your body shifts the goal from "perfect" to "healthy and thankful."

Reflection Question: What will you thank God for about your body today, and how will you treat it kindly?

Day 187

"God is in the midst of her; she shall not be moved." — Psalm 46:5a (KJV)

This verse feels like a hand on your back. God is with you—in the kitchen rush, the office tension, the doctor's waiting room. "Not moved" doesn't mean never rattled; it means not uprooted. Like a tree with deep roots, you can sway without snapping. Your steadiness isn't from willpower; it's from His presence. When worry tries to shove you, whisper, "He's here, I'm held." That's holy stubbornness.

Reflection Question: What moment today could change if you remembered, "God is in the midst of me"?

Day 188

"Two are better than one... For if they fall, the one will lift up his fellow." — Ecclesiastes 4:9-10a (KJV)

Sisterhood is God's idea. Better than one means better together—sharing errands, swapping stories, laughing ugly, crying honest. When you fall, a friend holds out a hand and reminds you who you are. Independence looks strong; interdependence is stronger. Friendship takes small risks: an invite, a follow-up text, a porch chat. Over time, those little yeses weave safety nets that hold on hard days.

Reflection Question: Who could you lift today—with a check-in, a ride, or a warm cup and a listening ear?

Day 189

"But let every man prove his own work, and then shall he have rejoicing in himself alone, and not in another." — Galatians 6:4 (KJV)

Comparison shrinks joy. Proving your own work looks like staying in your lane—running your race, not hers. That friend's promotion, that mom's craftiness, that woman's fitness routine—they're not your report card. Rejoicing in your work is noticing where God has you and being faithful there. Measure progress by obedience and growth, not likes or applause. Freedom returns when you cheer others and keep your eyes on your assignment.

Reflection Question: Where are you tempted to compare, and what truth will help you stay in your lane?

Day 190

"A soft answer turneth away wrath: but grievous words stir up anger." — Proverbs 15:1 (KJV)

Tone can turn a fight into a conversation. Soft doesn't mean weak; it means wise. A gentle answer lowers the volume so hearts can hear. Before replying, try a pause, a breath, a prayer. Ask, "What do I want to grow here—connection or distance?" Soft words are seeds that grow peace. Harsh ones grow walls. You get to choose which garden you'll plant.

Reflection Question: Which situation today needs a soft answer that turns heat into light?

Day 191

"...given to hospitality." — Romans 12:13b (KJV)

Hospitality isn't a Pinterest board; it's making room. A spare chair, a simple meal, a front porch swing can be holy. People don't remember your menu as much as your warmth. Summer makes it easier—paper plates, lemonade, yard chairs. Welcoming others is a way of saying, "You matter here." When you open your door, you open your heart, and God often meets you both.

Reflection Question: What simple welcome could you offer this week to make someone feel seen?

Day 192

"He shall gently lead those that are with young." — Isaiah 40:11b (KJV)

For moms, aunties, mentors, and caregivers—God sees your slow steps. He leads gently, not with hurry or harshness. He knows the 2 a.m. wakeups, the toddler meltdowns, the teen questions, the aging parent calls. Gentle leadership gives yourself the same grace you give others. Small routines count—songs at bedtime, prayers in the car line, hugs at the door. God's pace is kind, and He's proud to walk with you.

Reflection Question: Where can you mirror God's gentle lead in your care for others—and for yourself?

Day 193

"And whatsoever ye do, do it heartily, as to the Lord," — Colossians 3:23a (KJV)

Work looks like a lot of things—spreadsheets, diapers, sales calls, lesson plans, care tasks. Doing it "as to the Lord" lifts it from grind to gift. Heartily doesn't mean frantic; it means wholehearted—present, honest, faithful. Picture handing your task to Jesus: "This is for You." It changes your pace and your posture. Even unseen work shines when you remember who notices.

Reflection Question: What task will you hand to Jesus and do wholeheartedly for Him today?

Day 194

"My voice shalt thou hear in the morning, O LORD; in the morning will I direct my prayer unto thee," — Psalm 5:3a (KJV)

Morning prayers are like setting your GPS before driving. You aim your heart before the day pulls you. It doesn't have to be long—just honest. "Good morning, Lord. Lead me." The day still holds surprises, but your soul has a starting point. Prayer becomes a thread you tug on at noon and night, pulling you back to Him whenever you drift.

Reflection Question: What simple morning prayer will aim your heart toward God today?

Day 195

"The ornament of a meek and quiet spirit, which is in the sight of God of great price." — 1 Peter 3:4b (KJV)

Gentleness is not shrinking; it's strength under peace. A quiet spirit isn't silent; it's settled—rooted in God's love. This beauty doesn't fade or follow trends. It walks into a room without needing to prove, and leads without shouting. Meekness is like velvet over steel—soft to the touch, strong underneath. God prizes that kind of woman, and He loves to grow it in us.

Reflection Question: Where could a settled, gentle spirit become your quiet strength today?

Day 196

"I will instruct thee and teach thee... I will guide thee with mine eye." — Psalm 32:8 (KJV)

God's guidance isn't a scavenger hunt; it's a Father's eyes watching with care. He teaches through Scripture, nudges in prayer, wise friends, and holy common sense. Guidance with His eye feels personal—He knows your history, capacity, and calling. You don't need the year's map; you need today's step. Stay close enough to catch His glance, and you'll know when to move or wait.

Reflection Question: What decision needs you to slow down and look for God's guiding eyes?

Day 197

"But seek ye first the kingdom of God, and his righteousness; and all these things shall be added unto you." — Matthew 6:33 (KJV)

When bills, budgets, and needs swirl, Jesus reorders the list: first, the kingdom. Put God's priorities at the top—honesty, generosity, love—and watch how provision meets you. Seeking first looks practical: tithing before shopping, integrity before shortcuts, people before platform. God isn't stingy; He's wise. He adds what you need as you put Him first. That swap—from worry to worship—brings surprising peace.

Reflection Question: What "first" choice will you make today to trust God with the "added" things?

Day 198

"But let your communication be, Yea, yea; Nay, nay:" — Matthew 5:37a (KJV)

Clear yeses and nos are kindness. You don't have to explain away your limits. Simple honesty builds trust—with others and with yourself. A clean yes means you'll show up; a clean no means you won't resent the yes you shouldn't have given. Boundaries aren't unloving; they make love sustainable. Think: fewer maybes, more truth in love.

Reflection Question: Where do you need a clean yes or a kind no so your love can stay honest?

Day 199

"He hath sent me to bind up the brokenhearted..." — Isaiah 61:1b (KJV)

Jesus tends to hearts like a careful medic. Binding up doesn't rush; it cleans, wraps, and checks back in. If your heart feels cracked from betrayal, loss, or disappointment, you're not left to fix it alone. Healing takes time, truth, and tenderness. Let Jesus touch the tender places. He'll bandage you with His Word, surround you with people who care, and lead you into fresh hope.

Reflection Question: What tender place will you let Jesus tend, instead of toughing it out alone?

Day 200

"Yet I will rejoice in the LORD, I will joy in the God of my salvation."
— Habakkuk 3:18 (KJV)

"Yet" is defiant joy. When the pantry is thin, the inbox heavy, or the plan delayed, "yet" says, "God is still good." Joy isn't denial; it's decision. It looks like a small celebration: a walk at sunset, a song in the kitchen, a "thank You" whispered in traffic. The circumstance may not shift, but your spirit does. That move—from gloom to gratitude—opens space for hope to breathe.

Reflection Question: What is your "yet" today—one reason to rejoice in God right where you are?

Day 201

"Thine ears shall hear a word behind thee, saying, This is the way, walk ye in it," — Isaiah 30:21a (KJV)

God's guidance often sounds like a quiet nudge more than a loud horn. As you move, you sense, "Yes, this way," or, "Not that." Keep your pace slow enough to listen. He speaks through Scripture first, then confirms through peace, wise counsel, and providence. If you're torn between good options, ask for that behind-you whisper. He knows the turns ahead and how to get you there.

Reflection Question: Where do you need to slow enough to hear God's "this is the way" nudge?

Day 202

"Wait on the LORD: be of good courage, and he shall strengthen thine heart:" — Psalm 27:14a (KJV)

Waiting isn't wasted when it's with God. Courage grows in the pause. He strengthens hearts that refuse to grasp control and choose to trust instead. Waiting might look like not texting first, not forcing the door, not grabbing the cheaper integrity. The strength you gain in the wait will carry you when the yes arrives. Let hope sit beside you and hold your hand.

Reflection Question: What are you waiting on, and how will you let God strengthen your heart in it?

Day 203

"[Love] beareth all things, believeth all things, hopeth all things, endureth all things." — 1 Corinthians 13:7 (KJV)

Real love has backbone. It carries, trusts, hopes, and sticks around. This isn't about tolerating harm; it's about choosing a posture that protects and believes the best when possible. In marriage, friendship, family, and church, that kind of love makes safe places for growth. It says, "I'm for you," even while naming truth. Love is soft edges and strong center—both needed, both holy.

Reflection Question: Where can you add one ounce of "bear, believe, hope, endure" to your love today?

Day 204

"The inhabitants of the villages ceased... until that I Deborah arose, that I arose a mother in Israel." — Judges 5:7 (KJV)

Leadership often looks maternal—protective, wise, steady. Deborah stood up and things started moving. You don't need a title to lead; you need a willing heart. Step in with a solution, start the prayer, call the meeting, host the table. Leadership as a woman isn't shouting; it's shepherding. Rise where God nudges you. Your "yes" might wake a whole village.

Reflection Question: Where is God prompting you to "arise," and what first step can you take?

Day 205

"And the peace of God, which passeth all understanding, shall keep your hearts and minds through Christ Jesus." — Philippians 4:7 (KJV)

Some peace makes no sense on paper—and that's the point. God's peace stands guard like a night watch around your heart and mind. You may still feel waves, but you won't be swept away. This peace comes after prayer and trust, but it's a gift, not a grind. When anxiety knocks again, let peace answer the door with Jesus' name on its badge.

Reflection Question: What worry will you hand to God and welcome His guarding peace over?

Day 206

"Cast not away therefore your confidence, which hath great recompence of reward." — Hebrews 10:35 (KJV)

Confidence isn't swagger; it's settled trust in God and His calling on you. Don't toss it when doors take longer or critics get loud. Confidence keeps you showing up with a clear "I am His, and this is my lane." In time, that steadiness bears fruit—impact, joy, stories only God could write. Hold onto your confidence like a favorite jacket on a windy day.

Reflection Question: Where are you tempted to throw away confidence, and what truth will help you keep it on?

Day 207

"As every man hath received the gift, even so minister the same one to another," — 1 Peter 4:10a (KJV)

Gifts are for giving. God placed something in you—organization, encouragement, creativity, hospitality, teaching—that others need. Serving from overflow means you offer what you actually have, not what looks impressive. Start small and close: your church, your block, your group chat. God multiplies loaves and fishes; He can multiply your yes too.

Reflection Question: What gift will you share this week, right where you are?

Day 208

"So teach us to number our days, that we may apply our hearts unto wisdom." — Psalm 90:12 (KJV)

Summer fills fast. Wisdom numbers days not to stress, but to savor. You can't do everything, but you can do the right things—unhurried dinners, unhurried prayers, unhurried laughs. Numbering days helps you say no without guilt and yes without hurry. Time is a gift; spend it like someone who knows its value.

Reflection Question: What can you choose or release so your limited days hold what matters?

Day 209

"When I call to remembrance the unfeigned faith... which dwelt first in thy grandmother Lois, and thy mother Eunice;" — 2 Timothy 1:5a (KJV)

Faith runs in families and friendships. Maybe your grandma prayed you here. Maybe you're the first link in a new chain. Influence doesn't need a stage; it needs a kitchen table and a consistent life. Tell the stories. Say the prayers. Share the verses. The faith in you can lodge in others and live long past you.

Reflection Question: Who are you quietly shaping, and what faith seed can you plant today?

Day 210

"Put on the whole armour of God, that ye may be able to stand against the wiles of the devil." — Ephesians 6:11 (KJV)

Some days feel like a battle because they are. Armor up doesn't mean harden up; it means suit up—truth, righteousness, readiness, faith, salvation, the Word. These aren't props; they protect. Standing looks like refusing the lie, answering with Scripture, choosing peace shoes instead of anger spikes. God's armor fits women, too—strong, steady, beautiful in battle.

Reflection Question: Which piece of God's armor do you need most today, and how will you "put it on"?

Day 211

"...for man looketh on the outward appearance, but the LORD looketh on the heart." — 1 Samuel 16:7b (KJV)

The world grades the outside—clothes, skin, rooms, feeds. God sees the inside—courage, kindness, repentance, faith. That's both freeing and focusing. Care for your outside, sure, but invest most in your heart. Clean motives, quick forgiveness, secret prayers—these are stunning to God. When you feel overlooked, remember the One who chooses from the inside out.

Reflection Question: What heart-quality will you cultivate today that God delights to see?

Day 212

"There is therefore now no condemnation to them which are in Christ Jesus," — Romans 8:1a (KJV)

Condemnation says, "Guilty, always." The gospel says, "Forgiven, now." Shame wants you to wear old mistakes like a name tag; Jesus hands you a new one—Loved, Covered, Free. Conviction is different; it points to change with hope. Condemnation just points at you with accusation. In Christ, the courtroom is closed. You can walk forward light, not because you never stumbled, but because He stood up for you.

Reflection Question: What accusation will you refuse today, standing in the no-condemnation of Christ?

August: Wisdom, Prayer, and Everyday Faith

Day 213

"If any of you lack wisdom, let him ask of God... and it shall be given him." — James 1:5 (KJV)

Some decisions feel like standing at a four-way stop with cars coming from every direction—career shifts, school choices, family needs. God invites you to ask for wisdom, not once, but as often as the light changes. He gives generously, without rolling His eyes. Wisdom usually arrives in layers: a verse that stands out, a nudge that won't leave, counsel from a trusted friend, a holy "wait." You don't have to know the entire route to move. God's guidance shows up like headlights—enough for the next few feet. Ask, receive, step, repeat. That rhythm builds a life that's both practical and peaceful.

Reflection Question: Which decision needs you to simply ask God for wisdom and take the next small, faithful step?

Day 214

"The steps of a good man are ordered by the LORD: and he delighteth in his way." — Psalm 37:23 (KJV)

God orders steps, not just leaps. That's good news when life feels more like errands than epic moments. The appointment, the phone call, the grocery run—He can weave purpose into all of it. Ordered doesn't mean easy; it means arranged with care. Imagine a well-planned day planner, but written by Someone who knows tomorrow too. When plans change, you're not off His map. He delights in your way—not only the destination. Your ordinary path is sacred ground because He walks it with you.

Reflection Question: How will remembering that God orders your steps change the way you move through today's routine?

Day 215

"In all thy ways acknowledge him, and he shall direct thy paths." — Proverbs 3:6 (KJV)

Acknowledging God is more than a quick nod before meals; it's inviting Him into every lane. "All thy ways" includes budgets, calendars, texts, and tough talks. Direction often follows attention. When you pause—"Lord, be in this"—you make space for God to align your pace and your choices. Think of tapping your phone's compass; suddenly, you know which way is north. A simple habit of acknowledging Him shifts confusion to clarity, pressure to partnership.

Reflection Question: Where can you add a small "Lord, be in this" today so your path can settle under His direction?

Day 216

"Ask, and it shall be given you; seek, and ye shall find; knock, and it shall be opened unto you." — Matthew 7:7 (KJV)

Prayer has motion: ask, seek, knock. Sometimes it's a whisper; sometimes it's a search; sometimes it's persistent knocking when the door seems stuck. God isn't playing hard to get; He's drawing you close. Answers may look different than you imagined—strength instead of shortcuts, wisdom instead of wishes—but they arrive. Keep moving. Questions are not signs of weak faith; they're steps toward a faithful God.

Reflection Question: Which posture do you need today—asking, seeking, or knocking—and what will that look like?

Day 217

"Call unto me, and I will answer thee, and show thee great and mighty things..." — Jeremiah 33:3 (KJV)

God's line is never busy. "Call" sounds simple because it is. In the car, on a walk, between meetings—He welcomes your voice. Answers may be immediate or slow-grown, but this promise stands: He will answer and show. "Great and mighty things" aren't always flashy; sometimes they're a settled heart, a reconciled friendship, a wise no. Expect God to surprise you with the quality of His answers, not just the speed.

Reflection Question: What will you bring to God on the line today, trusting Him to answer in His wise way?

Day 218

"Teach me thy way, O LORD, and lead me in a plain path, because of mine enemies." — Psalm 27:11 (KJV)

Complicated days make a "plain path" sound like a miracle. David asks God to teach and lead, not just fix. A plain path is clear enough to walk without tripping over fear or overthinking. God's ways are learnable—humility, honesty, mercy, courage. He can simplify the tangled: one conversation at a time, one boundary at a time, one yes or no at a time. Ask for the next clear line, and trust Him to draw it.

Reflection Question: Where do you need God to make the next step plain—and will you take it when it's clear?

Day 219

"The fear of the LORD is the beginning of wisdom:" — Proverbs 9:10a (KJV)

Wisdom starts with awe, not answers. When God is big in your view, problems shrink to their true size. Fear here isn't panic; it's reverence—treating God as God. It looks like checking your motives, honoring what He says even when it's hard, and trusting His character when you don't get His timing. Start the day by lifting your eyes: "You are God, I am not." That posture sets the table for wise choices.

Reflection Question: How might a fresh reverence for God reframe a decision that's been stressing you?

Day 220

"Commit thy works unto the LORD, and thy thoughts shall be established." — Proverbs 16:3 (KJV)

Commit the work, and watch your thoughts settle. Anxiety often races when tasks feel ownerless. Hand the project, the parenting, the shift at work to God—out loud if it helps. When He carries the weight, your mind stops spinning and starts focusing. Established thoughts are like a sturdy bookshelf; your ideas have somewhere to sit without collapsing. Work becomes worship, and clarity follows commitment.

Reflection Question: What piece of work will you commit to the Lord so your thoughts can find steady ground?

Day 221

"Continue in prayer, and watch in the same with thanksgiving;" — Colossians 4:2 (KJV)

Two hands of prayer: persistence and watchfulness. Keep praying, and keep your eyes open for small answers. Thanksgiving tunes your attention—suddenly you see the text that was timely, the door that cracked open, the strength that wasn't there yesterday. Continuing doesn't mean begging; it means staying in conversation. Watching keeps you from missing what you prayed for.

Reflection Question: What ongoing prayer will you keep before God, and where are you seeing early answers?

Day 222

"Be not wise in thine own eyes: fear the LORD, and depart from evil."
— *Proverbs 3:7 (KJV)*

Our eyes lie sometimes—especially when pride puts a filter on them. Being "wise in your own eyes" is refusing input, skipping prayer, or explaining away red flags. Wisdom welcomes correction and takes sin seriously because it harms. Departing from evil can be as practical as unfollowing a feed, changing a route, or confessing quickly. Humility is protective—it keeps you teachable and safe.

Reflection Question: Where might you be relying on your own eyes, and what humble step could realign you with God?

Day 223

"Set your affection on things above, not on things on the earth." —
Colossians 3:2 (KJV)

Affection is attention with love. Where you set it shapes your day. Things above look like Jesus' priorities—people over platform, character over image, truth over convenience. This doesn't ignore bills and chores; it orders them under a bigger love. It's the difference between scrolling for escape and pausing to pray for the person you just saw. Setting your affection higher lifts your mood and your mission.

Reflection Question: What will you move from "earth" to "above" in your heart today so your focus fits Jesus?

Day 224

"Thy word is a lamp unto my feet, and a light unto my path." — Psalm 119:105 (KJV)

You don't need stadium lights; you need a lamp for your feet. God's Word illuminates the next few steps—enough to keep you from stumbling. Read a little, walk a little, repeat. Over time, the path brightens. When choices feel murky, go back to what's clear: love God, love people, tell the truth, keep your promise, choose kindness. Scripture makes complicated seasons navigable, one verse at a time.

Reflection Question: What small portion of God's Word will you carry like a lamp into today's choices?

Day 225

"A man's heart deviseth his way: but the LORD directeth his steps." — Proverbs 16:9 (KJV)

Plan your way; hold it loosely. God directs in motion. You mark the calendar, craft the list, then stay interruptible. Divine detours sometimes look like delays, but they often hide kindness—avoiding harm, meeting a need, teaching patience. Trust the Director more than the plan. He cares more about who you become on the way than how fast you arrive.

Reflection Question: Where can you stay flexible today so God can redirect your good plans if He wants?

Day 226

"Pray without ceasing." — 1 Thessalonians 5:17 (KJV)

Unceasing prayer sounds impossible until you think of it as constant connection. Like keeping a text thread open with a best friend, you check in throughout the day—thanks, help, wow, sorry. Breath prayers count. "Lord, have mercy." "Jesus, be near." "Thank You." This doesn't replace quiet time; it threads prayer through everything else, stitching your day together with grace.

Reflection Question: What short prayer will you return to on repeat so your heart stays connected to God?

Day 227

"He that walketh with wise men shall be wise: but a companion of fools shall be destroyed." — Proverbs 13:20 (KJV)

Your people shape your path. Walk with wisdom—friends who tell you truth kindly, who pray more than they gossip, who celebrate without envy. You become like those you linger with. That doesn't mean ditch hard friendships; it means anchor yourself to wise ones so you're not swept away by foolishness. Choose tables that feed your soul, not just your appetite for drama.

Reflection Question: Who are your wise walkers, and how will you lean into their influence this week?

Day 228

"Trust in the LORD with all thine heart; and lean not unto thine own understanding." — Proverbs 3:5 (KJV)

Understanding wants the driver's seat; trust asks it to slide over. You don't ignore your brain—you just refuse to make it your god. God sees angles you can't: timing, motives, outcomes. Leaning on Him looks like obeying before you fully "get it," forgiving when it feels risky, waiting when hurry screams go. Trust takes practice, but peace grows with it.

Reflection Question: Where are you leaning hard on understanding, and how could trust lead you differently?

Day 229

"Be careful for nothing; but in every thing by prayer... with thanksgiving let your requests be made known unto God." — Philippians 4:6 (KJV)

Worry writes long lists at 2 a.m. Prayer writes them too—then hands them over. Thanksgiving keeps panic from holding the pen. Be specific: names, deadlines, needs. God isn't annoyed by details; He's invited by them. As you trade rumination for conversation, heaviness lifts. The situation may still be complex, but your heart won't carry it solo.

Reflection Question: What one worry will you turn into a specific, thankful prayer today?

Day 230

"He shall direct thy paths." — *Proverbs 3:6b (KJV)*

God's direction is both firm and kind. When you veer, He nudges. When you stall, He prompts. Sometimes He blocks a path you wanted because another road leads to life. Look back and you'll see His fingerprints—closed doors that saved you, open ones you never could have forced, surprising turns that grew you up. Keep your hands on the wheel and your heart tuned to His voice.

Reflection Question: What recent "nudge" felt like God directing, and how will you respond today?

Day 231

"The effectual fervent prayer of a righteous man availeth much." —
James 5:16b (KJV)

Prayer works—not because of volume, but because of the One who listens. Effectual and fervent sound big, but they can be simple: sincere, persistent, aligned with God's heart. Think of a steady drip filling a bucket. Over time, the bucket moves. Keep dripping. Pray Scripture back to God. Keep short accounts with sin. Love people while you pray for them. That combination "availeth much."

Reflection Question: Who or what will you pray for steadily, trusting God to do what only He can?

Day 232

"A wise man will hear, and will increase learning;" — *Proverbs 1:5a (KJV)*

Wisdom listens first. Not to respond, but to understand. It asks good questions and admits when it doesn't know. Increase learning might look like reading a chapter, seeking advice, observing before deciding. This posture keeps you from preventable mistakes and opens doors you didn't even know existed. Curiosity under the fear of God is a superpower.

Reflection Question: Where could better listening be your wisest move today?

Day 233

"He that keepeth his mouth keepeth his life: but he that openeth wide his lips shall have destruction." — *Proverbs 13:3 (KJV)*

Words build or break. Keeping your mouth can save a friendship, a job, a marriage. Biting your tongue isn't weakness; it's wisdom when emotions are hot. Before you post or press send, ask if your words are true, kind, and needed. Silence can be a strong answer; restraint can be holy. Later, when your heart is cooler, your words will be better.

Reflection Question: What conversation or comment needs restraint from you so life—not damage—can result?

Day 234

"Evening, and morning, and at noon, will I pray, and cry aloud: and he shall hear my voice." — Psalm 55:17 (KJV)

Bookend your day with prayer, and drop a prayer in the middle. It's like meals for your soul—regular nourishment keeps you steady. Evening releases what you carried. Morning sets your aim. Noon re-centers you before the afternoon sprint. This rhythm isn't rigid; it's relational. God hears every time—whispers and cries alike.

Reflection Question: Which mealtime of prayer—morning, noon, or evening—will you commit to today so your heart stays nourished?

Day 235

"He will guide you into all truth." — John 16:13b (KJV)

Truth isn't just a concept; it's a path. The Spirit guides—He doesn't shove. He leads you into truth about God, about yourself, about others. Sometimes that truth comforts; sometimes it corrects. Both are grace. If confusion has been loud, ask the Spirit to bring clarity. He loves to spotlight Jesus and straighten what's crooked in your thinking.

Reflection Question: Where do you need the Spirit's gentle guidance into truth that frees and clarifies?

Day 236

"Keep thy heart with all diligence; for out of it are the issues of life." —
Proverbs 4:23 (KJV)

Your heart is the spring that feeds everything else. Guard it like you would a fresh well—keep trash out, keep water flowing. Diligence looks like boundaries on what you watch, honesty about jealousy, quick forgiveness before bitterness hardens. When the well is clear, life tastes different—kinder words, cleaner motives, steadier emotions. Protecting your heart protects your life.

Reflection Question: What one guardrail could help keep your heart clear and healthy this week?

Day 237

"Continue instant in prayer;" — *Romans 12:12c (KJV)*

Instant means ready at any moment—like keeping a kettle warm. Prayer doesn't need fancy words or perfect timing. It needs availability. When you hear a siren, pray. When a name pops up, pray. When joy hits, thank Him. This responsiveness builds a reflex that keeps you close to God and attentive to people. It's simple, and it changes rooms.

Reflection Question: What everyday cue will you link with a quick prayer so your reflex turns toward God?

Day 238

"He restoreth my soul: he leadeth me in the paths of righteousness for his name's sake." — Psalm 23:3 (KJV)

Restoration and righteousness travel together. God doesn't just patch you up; He leads you into better paths. Soul care isn't only bubble baths—it's also better choices: healthier boundaries, honest conversations, real rest. He restores as He redirects. And it's for His name's sake—your healing tells the truth about His goodness. Let Him shepherd you toward places that strengthen you.

Reflection Question: What restorative choice will you make today that also aligns with God's right path?

Day 239

"In the multitude of counsellors there is safety." — Proverbs 11:14b (KJV)

Big decisions need more than gut feelings. Invite a few wise voices—diverse, godly, honest. Safety doesn't mean you'll avoid all risk; it means you'll avoid avoidable mistakes. Let others see your blind spots and ask hard questions. Counsel protects dreams from drifting into folly and keeps fear from shrinking good plans. You don't have to figure it out solo.

Reflection Question: Who are the two or three counselors you can ask for input on your next decision?

Day 240

"Draw nigh to God, and he will draw nigh to you." — James 4:8a (KJV)

God moves toward movers. A step toward Him—five quiet minutes, a whispered song, an open Bible—meets His eager nearness. You won't always feel fireworks; sometimes it's a quiet sense that you're not alone. The promise stands: draw near, and He draws near. He loves your reach, however small.

Reflection Question: What simple step toward God will you take today, trusting He'll meet you there?

Day 241

"Be swift to hear, slow to speak, slow to wrath:" — James 1:19b (KJV)

Speed matters. Quick ears, slow mouth, slower anger—that order saves relationships. Listening first doesn't mean you agree; it means you value. Speaking slowly lets wisdom catch up to emotion. Slow anger protects your health and your words from becoming weapons. Try a pause that lasts three breaths; you'll be amazed what stays unsaid—and how peace grows.

Reflection Question: Which situation today needs you to switch gears: faster listening, slower talking, or slower anger?

Day 242

"The prudent man foreseeth the evil, and hideth himself; but the simple pass on, and are punished." — Proverbs 27:12 (KJV)

Prudence isn't fear; it's foresight. You spot a red flag and take cover—budget before the bill, rest before burnout, boundaries before regret. Hiding yourself looks like wisdom-driven choices, not shrinking back from life. Godly caution protects joy. The simple keep marching into messes; the prudent make a turn. Look ahead with the Spirit's help and choose the safer lane.

Reflection Question: What small, prudent adjustment today could save you from a bigger problem later?

Day 243

"Blessed is the man that heareth me, watching daily at my gates, waiting at the posts of my doors." — Proverbs 8:34 (KJV)

Wisdom keeps office hours. "Watching daily" paints a picture of someone showing up at God's door ready to learn. It's unhurried, faithful, expectant. You won't always leave with fireworks, but you'll leave with direction. Daily watching builds a life that doesn't panic when pressure comes, because you've been listening all along. Blessing lives in that rhythm—steady, quiet, strong.

Reflection Question: How will you "watch daily" for God's wisdom—at a set time, in a set place—so blessing can grow?

September: New Rhythms, Steady Hearts

Day 244

"To every thing there is a season, and a time to every purpose under the heaven." — *Ecclesiastes 3:1 (KJV)*

September feels like fresh notebooks and new calendars. Life shifts gears—school starts, routines return, daylight shortens. God isn't surprised by any season; He authors them. Some months are for planting, some for pruning, some for resting. Trying to force summer pace into fall can leave you frazzled. Let the new rhythm be a friend, not a foe. Ask, "What belongs in this season—and what doesn't?" Think sweaters replacing sandals: different isn't worse, just different. When you match your steps to God's timing, peace rises. Purpose doesn't get lost when routines change; often it gets clearer.

Reflection Question: What one adjustment could help your September rhythm align with God's season for you?

Day 245

"My presence shall go with thee, and I will give thee rest." — Exodus 33:14 (KJV)

New schedules can make your shoulders tight. God answers with presence, not just productivity tips. "I'm with you" is better than "try harder." Rest here doesn't mean doing nothing; it means doing life with Someone. Imagine walking into the meeting or the pickup line knowing you're not alone—your pace softens, your tone gentles. Presence changes atmosphere. You don't have to curate calm; you can carry it because He carries you. When your day stacks up like heavy books, slide this promise underneath as the shelf that holds the weight.

Reflection Question: Where do you need to remember, "He is with me," so rest can slip into your day?

Day 246

"Casting all your care upon him; for he careth for you." — 1 Peter 5:7 (KJV)

Casting isn't delicate; it's a throw. Picture tossing a backpack onto stronger shoulders. Worry doesn't make you more responsible; it makes you more tired. God invites you to fling the concerns—tuition, test results, tension at work—onto Him. Care is not a general concept; it's personal. He cares for you, by name, with detail. You may need to cast repeatedly as the load tries to climb back on. That's okay. Keep throwing it His way and walking lighter.

Reflection Question: What burden will you toss onto God today instead of quietly carrying alone?

Day 247

"Let your light so shine before men... and glorify your Father which is in heaven." — Matthew 5:16 (KJV)

Light doesn't perform; it simply shines. In a world that sometimes feels dim, your everyday kindness is bright—returning the cart, sending the text, staying gentle in a hard thread. You don't have to be loud to be luminous. Your good works point past you to a good Father. Like a porch light that guides people home, your life can help others find their way to Him.

Reflection Question: Where can your quiet light make a hallway, a home, or a heart a little brighter today?

Day 248

"He that is faithful in that which is least is faithful also in much." — Luke 16:10a (KJV)

Big dreams grow in small soil. Faithfulness looks like proofreading the email, showing up on time, finishing what you start. No spotlight, just steady. God notices. The "least" places are training grounds where character builds muscle. Think of reps at the gym—you don't see change in one session, but strength is forming. When larger opportunities come, you'll be ready because small ones shaped you.

Reflection Question: What simple task can you treat with "big" faithfulness today?

Day 249

"Thou wilt keep him in perfect peace, whose mind is stayed on thee: because he trusteth in thee." — Isaiah 26:3 (KJV)

Peace isn't found by scrolling; it's found by staying. A stayed mind returns to God like a screensaver returning to calm. Trust shifts your gaze from "what if" to "who is." Perfect peace doesn't mean perfect circumstances; it means a settled heart in the middle of them. Try short returns throughout the day: breathe, speak His name, remember a verse. Little re-centers lead to lasting peace.

Reflection Question: What simple "return to God" habit could keep your mind stayed on Him today?

Day 250

"Humble yourselves in the sight of the Lord, and he shall lift you up." — James 4:10 (KJV)

Humility isn't thinking less of yourself; it's thinking of yourself less. It looks like listening first, admitting limits, and giving credit away. In a season of fresh starts, humility keeps you teachable—new roles, new routines, new grace. God does the lifting; you don't have to elbow your way up. In His timing, He places you where your gifts serve best.

Reflection Question: Where could humility open a door for God to do the lifting instead of you?

Day 251

"There are many devices in a man's heart; nevertheless the counsel of the LORD, that shall stand." — Proverbs 19:21 (KJV)

You can sketch plans in pencil; God holds the pen. Devices (ideas) multiply—calendars, budgets, goals. Make them, yes—but hold them lightly. God's counsel isn't a last-minute edit; it's the foundation. When plans shift, it's not always failure; sometimes it's favor, steering you to better. Look back and notice where His standing counsel outlasted your best ideas. That memory builds trust for the next change.

Reflection Question: What plan will you hold with open hands so God's counsel can stand in front?

Day 252

"Let the word of Christ dwell in you richly..." — Colossians 3:16a (KJV)

Rich dwelling is more than a quick visit. Let Scripture take up space—on your lips, in your car, around your table. Songs count, verses taped to mirrors count, a chapter before bed counts. The Word becomes the house rules for your heart: how you speak, choose, forgive. When life knocks, what's inside comes out; let it be truth that steadies and sings.

Reflection Question: What simple way will you let God's Word "move in" a little more richly this week?

Day 253

"I will bless the LORD at all times: his praise shall continually be in my mouth." — Psalm 34:1 (KJV)

All times includes Mondays, traffic, and tense emails. Continual praise doesn't ignore hard stuff; it names God's goodness alongside it. A whispered "thank You" in the grocery aisle recalibrates your mood. Praise in the small moments keeps your heart from slipping into complaint. Over time, gratitude becomes your default setting.

Reflection Question: Where can praise share space with your stress so your mouth tells the truer story?

Day 254

"For even the Son of man came not to be ministered unto, but to minister," — Mark 10:45a (KJV)

If anyone deserved to be served, it was Jesus—yet He washed feet and set tables. Serving doesn't shrink you; it shapes you like Him. It may look like refilling waters at dinner, covering a shift, or staying late to help a teammate. Service turns ordinary places into holy ground. You'll notice joy sneaking in when you make someone else's load a little lighter.

Reflection Question: What small act of service can you offer that makes someone's day easier?

Day 255

"Be not forgetful to entertain strangers: for thereby some have entertained angels unawares." — Hebrews 13:2 (KJV)

Hospitality starts with noticing. The new face at church, the neighbor on a walk, the student far from home—welcome makes people breathe easier. You don't need a perfect house; you need a warm yes. Paper plates work. A porch works. God seems to tuck surprises into simple hospitality—friendships you didn't see coming, joy you can't plan. Who knows what you'll host when you open the door?

Reflection Question: Who could you welcome this week with a simple, un-fancy invitation?

Day 256

"Be ye kind one to another, tenderhearted, forgiving one another, even as God for Christ's sake hath forgiven you." — Ephesians 4:32 (KJV)

Kindness is powerful in a sharp world. Tender hearts don't mean thin skin; they mean soft edges toward people who are also carrying something. Forgiveness frees both sides—it doesn't erase pain, but it clears the path for healing. When you remember how God forgave you, generosity rises. The circle completes: loved people love.

Reflection Question: Where can kindness or forgiveness soften a rough edge in your relationships today?

Day 257

"The integrity of the upright shall guide them:" — *Proverbs 11:3a (KJV)*

Integrity is a built-in compass. It simplifies choices: tell the truth, keep your word, do right when no one's looking. You'll sleep better. It may cost in the short term, but it pays in peace. In a season of new commitments, integrity keeps you from overpromising and underdelivering. Let who you are in private match who you are in public—steady, honest, whole.

Reflection Question: What decision could be simplified by choosing the honest, whole-hearted option?

Day 258

"What time I am afraid, I will trust in thee." — *Psalm 56:3 (KJV)*

Fear doesn't wait for convenient moments. It shows up at night or right before the presentation. This verse doesn't shame fear; it gives it a place to go—trust. Trust looks like, "God, I'm scared, but You're steady." Imagine sliding your trembling hand into His. Courage is fear with its hand in God's. You may still feel the wobble, but you won't be ruled by it.

Reflection Question: Where will you move forward afraid, choosing trust as your next step?

Day 259

"I exhort therefore, that, first of all, supplications, prayers... be made for all men; For kings, and for all that are in authority;" — 1 Timothy 2:1-2a (KJV)

We talk about leaders a lot; praying for them is quieter—and stronger. From school boards to supervisors to officials you didn't vote for, lift them up. God can steady hands that steer policies and workplaces. Prayer doesn't mean agreement; it means asking for wisdom, justice, and peace. It shapes your heart too, softening cynicism and growing hope.

Reflection Question: Which leader—local or national—will you pray for today, asking God to guide them wisely?

Day 260

"If we confess our sins, he is faithful and just to forgive us our sins, and to cleanse us..." — 1 John 1:9 (KJV)

Confession is not groveling; it's coming clean so you can breathe. God's faithfulness and justice are on your side because of Jesus. He doesn't dangle forgiveness like a carrot; He gives it. Cleansing goes beyond pardon—it removes the residue. Think of a spilled drink mopped up and the sticky gone. Your heart can feel like that—light, clear, ready to love again.

Reflection Question: What honest confession to God could clear space for fresh joy today?

Day 261

"The wisdom that is from above is first pure, then peaceable, gentle...
full of mercy and good fruits," — James 3:17 (KJV)

Heaven's wisdom has a flavor, and it's not harsh. It's clean, peace-making, considerate, merciful. When you're weighing a response or a decision, check the taste. If it's bitter, it's probably not from above. Wisdom isn't just about being right; it's about bringing peace and bearing fruit. Imagine conversations where gentleness and mercy lead—rooms change.

Reflection Question: What would "peaceable and gentle" look like in the next choice you make?

Day 262

"Death and life are in the power of the tongue:" — Proverbs 18:21a
(KJV)

Words carry weight. You've felt the sting and the lift. Today you'll speak life or drain it—over yourself, your kids, your coworkers. Life-words sound like encouragement, truth, blessing, boundaries with kindness. Before you deliver a sentence, ask, "Will this plant or poison?" You don't need fancy; you need sincere. Life grows where life is spoken.

Reflection Question: What life-giving sentence can you speak to someone (or yourself) today?

Day 263

"The sabbath was made for man, and not man for the sabbath:" —
Mark 2:27 (KJV)

Rest is a gift, not a guilt trip. God designed a rhythm where you stop and let the world spin without you. That's humbling and healing. Your worth doesn't shrink when your to-do list pauses. Sabbath can look like a tech-light afternoon, a slow meal, a nap, a walk that listens. When you rest, you say with your body, "God runs things. I trust Him."

Reflection Question: What restful practice could help your soul exhale this week?

Day 264

"Seest thou a man diligent in his business? he shall stand before kings;"
— Proverbs 22:29a (KJV)

Diligence is quiet excellence—showing up prepared, doing the work when no one's clapping. Over time, it opens doors you didn't even knock on. You don't chase platforms; you cultivate craft. Kings might be bosses, clients, or opportunities that require trust. Diligence says, "You can count on me," and people do.

Reflection Question: Where could a little extra care in your work today build future trust?

Day 265

"Commit thy way unto the LORD; trust also in him; and he shall bring it to pass." — Psalm 37:5 (KJV)

Commit is hands-open language—placing your route in God's. Trust holds steady when the timeline stretches. "Bring it to pass" may look different than you pictured, but it will be good. Think of mailing a package—you release it to a reliable carrier and stop worrying about the route. God's delivery is wiser and kinder than ours.

Reflection Question: What plan or hope will you hand over to God and trust Him to carry?

Day 266

"Let your speech be alway with grace, seasoned with salt," — Colossians 4:6a (KJV)

Grace is the main course; salt is the seasoning—truth with kindness that preserves the relationship. Words can be bland (avoiding truth) or too salty (burning people). Grace-salt balance tells the truth in a way people can receive. Before you hit send or speak up, ask if your words are edible—helpful, flavorful, and kind.

Reflection Question: Which conversation needs grace first and salt second so it nourishes, not harms?

Day 267

"The LORD is good, a strong hold in the day of trouble; and he knoweth them that trust in him." — Nahum 1:7 (KJV)

Trouble days don't change God's goodness; they reveal it. Stronghold sounds like thick walls and a safe room. Run there. He doesn't just guard a crowd; He knows those who trust Him—by name, by story. Knowing you're known steadies your breathing. You don't have to fake brave; you can rest behind His walls.

Reflection Question: Where will you step inside God's stronghold instead of bracing in your own strength?

Day 268

"I have learned, in whatsoever state I am, therewith to be content." — Philippians 4:11b (KJV)

Contentment is learned, not luck. Paul practiced it—highs and lows, plenty and little. Contentment doesn't cancel ambition; it anchors it. You can aim and still be grateful in the current chapter. Think of settling into the seat you have instead of standing in the aisle wishing for another. Peace grows when you bless the now while you build the next.

Reflection Question: What can you genuinely bless about your "now" while you work toward "next"?

Day 269

"The aged women likewise... teachers of good things;" — *Titus 2:3 (KJV)*

Generations need each other. Older women carry stories and steady wisdom; younger women bring energy and fresh eyes. Teaching "good things" happens around tables, in texts, on walks—sharing recipes, budget tips, prayer habits, hard-earned lessons. You don't need a podium; you need presence. Ask, listen, offer. Together, we grow stronger and kinder.

Reflection Question: Who across generations could you learn from—or encourage—with one simple connection?

Day 270

"My help cometh from the LORD, which made heaven and earth. He will not suffer thy foot to be moved:" — *Psalm 121:2-3a (KJV)*

Help is coming—from the Maker, not a middleman. When the hill ahead looks steep, remember whose hand you hold. "Not be moved" doesn't mean never stumble; it means not be toppled. Like good hiking boots on a rocky path, God's help keeps your footing. Look up before you look around; your help is higher than the mountain.

Reflection Question: Where do you need to lift your eyes and expect help that holds your steps?

Day 271

"Be kindly affectioned one to another with brotherly love; in honour preferring one another;" — Romans 12:10 (KJV)

Kind affection looks like warm eyes and small honors—letting someone go first, saving the last slice, choosing words that dignify. Preferring one another doesn't erase you; it enriches the room. In a culture of "me first," this is quietly radical. It builds families, teams, and churches that feel safe and strong.

Reflection Question: What simple honor can you give someone today to say, "You go first"?

Day 272

"A man hath joy by the answer of his mouth: and a word spoken in due season, how good is it!" — Proverbs 15:23 (KJV)

Right words at the right time feel like cool water on a hot day. Joy returns to the speaker too—encouragement blesses both sides. You don't need the perfect phrase; you need a timely, sincere one. Pay attention to nudges: text her now, speak up in the meeting, say "I'm proud of you." Due season words often arrive in simple sentences that linger long.

Reflection Question: Who might need a timely, good word from you before the day ends?

Day 273

"I have set before thee an open door, and no man can shut it:" —
Revelation 3:8a (KJV)

Open doors aren't always flashy; sometimes they're humble starts that fit your hands. God opens; you walk. No one can shut what He swings wide—not timelines, not opinions. Stay faithful where you are, and watch for the door with your name on it. When it opens, you won't need to force it; you'll need courage to step through.

Reflection Question: Where do you sense an open door—and what small, courageous step can you take through it?

October: Harvest of Trust and Steady Light

Day 274

"Be still, and know that I am God:" — Psalm 46:10 (KJV)

October invites slower evenings—earlier sunsets, warm mugs, softer schedules. "Be still" fits this season. Still doesn't mean stop everything; it means unclench inside. Like turning off a loud fan and realizing how quiet the house really is. In the hush, you remember: God is God, not you. He holds your people, your plans, your unknowns. Stillness makes faith audible. Try a small pause—phone facedown, a deep breath, a whispered, "You're here." The worries won't disappear, but they'll find their proper size. Knowing God grows best in unhurried moments, the kind with leaves falling and hearts listening.

Reflection Question: Where can you carve out a pocket of stillness today so you can know—not just know about—God?

Day 275

"I will never leave thee, nor forsake thee." — Hebrews 13:5b (KJV)

Shorter days can feel lonelier. The house gets quiet earlier; shadows stretch long. God's promise stands taller than the dark: I'm not leaving. He is not a flake or a phase. He's steady presence on the couch, in the car, at the sink. Sometimes you sense Him, sometimes you just trust Him—but either way, He's there. Picture a nightlight in a child's room—small, consistent, comforting. God's nearness is brighter than that. You're not carrying the evening alone, or the month, or the year. When your chest tightens, say it out loud: "You're with me."

Reflection Question: What ordinary moment today could change if you really believed God won't leave you there?

Day 276

"In all labour there is profit:" — Proverbs 14:23a (KJV)

This is mid-semester, mid-project, mid-pile-of-laundry season. The grind can feel thankless. God says your work counts. Not just the wins—the labor itself. Packing lunches, prepping slides, driving carpool, caring for patients, checking in on a neighbor—there's profit in the showing up. Think of a garden in October—roots thickening even when the flowers fade. Faithful effort builds invisible strength. Your hands may be tired, but they're building something: trust, skill, character, care. That's profit heaven loves to measure.

Reflection Question: Which humble task will you treat as meaningful today because God says it matters?

Day 277

"For God hath not given us the spirit of fear; but of power, and of love, and of a sound mind." — 2 Timothy 1:7 (KJV)

Anxious thoughts can stack like leaves in a gutter—suddenly everything feels flooded. Fear isn't your inheritance. God gives power to act, love to guide, and a sound mind to sort truth from noise. Power might be one email or one boundary. Love chooses people over panic. A sound mind asks, "Is this true? Is this mine to carry? What has God said?" Take a slow breath. Picture God handing you these three gifts, one by one. They fit your hands.

Reflection Question: What could change if you reached for power, love, and a sound mind instead of fear in one situation today?

Day 278

"O satisfy us early with thy mercy; that we may rejoice and be glad all our days." — Psalm 90:14 (KJV)

Morning mercy sets the tone. Before the inbox, before the news, drink the first cup from God's kindness. Early satisfaction isn't about schedule—it's about priority. When His mercy fills the first slot, rejoicing finds room in slots two through ten. Think of preheating the oven so everything bakes right. Mercy preheats your heart for the day's mix of sweet and salty. Start simple: "Thank You for new mercy. Help me notice it."

Reflection Question: What small morning habit could help you taste God's mercy before anything else?

Day 279

"Bear ye one another's burdens, and so fulfil the law of Christ." —
Galatians 6:2 (KJV)

Fall is casserole season—for the sick, the stressed, the new parents. Burden-bearing looks like meals, rides, a Venmo, a listening ear. You're not called to fix everything, just to shoulder a corner. Think of four friends carrying one mat; together, the weight moves. Christ's law is love, and love lifts. Your help might not be dramatic; it will be holy.

Reflection Question: Whose load feels heavy right now, and how can you help carry a corner of it?

Day 280

"I am the light of the world." — *John 8:12a (KJV)*

As days dim, lamps matter more. Jesus calls Himself Light in a world that stumbles. His light doesn't glare; it guides. Warm, steady, kind. When you don't know the next step, stand under His light—open the Gospels, pray a simple prayer, ask a wise friend. And then, let His light in you glow on others: a calm presence, a hopeful word, an honest "me too." Darkness can't out-argue light; it just leaves.

Reflection Question: Where do you need Jesus' light to guide you—and where can that light spill over to someone else?

Day 281

"O taste and see that the LORD is good:" — Psalm 34:8a (KJV)

Fall flavors are bold—spiced cider, roasted squash, warm bread. God invites you to taste His goodness, not just think about it. Taste is experiential: answered prayer, an unexpected check, laughter after tears, peace that doesn't make sense. Sometimes you have to take a bite—try obedience, risk kindness, show up to serve—and discover flavor you didn't expect. God's good isn't theoretical; it's edible.

Reflection Question: What step of faith could help you "taste" God's goodness in a real way this week?

Day 282

"Men ought always to pray, and not to faint;" — Luke 18:1b (KJV)

There's a special kind of tired that hits in October. Jesus says keep praying so you don't faint. Prayer is oxygen. Short, steady breaths—"Help," "Thanks," "Guide me," "Be near." Like a runner sipping water at mile eight, small prayers keep you moving. The point isn't eloquence; it's endurance. God hears the panting prayers and answers with enough strength for the next step.

Reflection Question: Where are you tempted to faint, and what simple prayer can keep you moving there?

Day 283

"Present your bodies a living sacrifice, holy, acceptable unto God, which is your reasonable service." — Romans 12:1b (KJV)

Living sacrifice sounds big, but it shows up small: offering your schedule, your mouth, your hands, your home. It's choosing God's way in traffic and at the table. Reasonable means it makes sense because of mercy. When you look at His love, offering yourself back feels like the natural response. Not a burnt offering—more like a daily "yes." Sacred, ordinary, repeated.

Reflection Question: What ordinary part of yourself will you offer to God today as a willing "yes"?

Day 284

"Let the words of my mouth, and the meditation of my heart, be acceptable in thy sight," — Psalm 19:14a (KJV)

Words and thoughts are roommates; they influence each other. If your mind loops on irritation, your mouth will leak it. Invite God into both spaces. Ask Him to tidy the inner conversation so the outer one blesses. Think of putting a screen over a drain—keeps the gunk from flowing out. Acceptable doesn't mean fake nice; it means true, kind, measured. Your heart gets lighter when your words get cleaner.

Reflection Question: What thought pattern could shift so your words line up with what pleases God?

Day 285

"Pleasant words are as an honeycomb, sweet to the soul, and health to the bones." — Proverbs 16:24 (KJV)

Honey calms a scratchy throat; kind words do the same for scratchy days. Pleasant doesn't mean empty flattery; it means true encouragement, gentle truth, sincere thanks. You've felt the lift—a boss's kind note, a friend's "I'm proud of you," a child's messy compliment. Sweetness and health—that's the power of well-timed words. Keep a small stash ready. You'll brighten rooms and bones.

Reflection Question: Who needs a honeyed word from you today, and what will you say?

Day 286

"What doth the LORD require of thee, but to do justly, and to love mercy, and to walk humbly with thy God?" — Micah 6:8b (KJV)

When life feels complicated, God simplifies: do justice, love mercy, walk humbly. Justice looks like fairness when no one's watching. Mercy loves to forgive and to help. Walking humbly keeps you teachable and kind. These aren't headlines; they're habits—how you tip, how you talk, how you treat the least noticeable person in the room. With God, small right things add up to a life that matters.

Reflection Question: Which of these three—justice, mercy, humility—needs more space in your steps today?

Day 287

"Do all things without murmurings and disputings:" — *Philippians 2:14 (KJV)*

Cool mornings can make grumbling easy—traffic, lines, chores. This verse isn't scolding; it's an invitation to a lighter heart. Complaining costs energy you could use for actual change or quiet joy. Try swapping the complaint with thanks or a constructive ask. Picture your words as either fogging the day or clearing it. Choose clear. You'll feel the difference before lunch.

Reflection Question: What common complaint can you trade for gratitude or a gracious request today?

Day 288

"Blessed is the man that trusteth in the LORD... For he shall be as a tree planted by the waters," — *Jeremiah 17:7-8a (KJV)*

Trees don't panic about weather; they dig roots. Trust is root work. When news cycles swirl and plans shift, planted people stay green. Watered trust looks like consistent prayer, Scripture in your ears, wise community, small obediences. Fruit doesn't show up every day, but health does—resilience, calm, steady hope. Plant by the Source, and watch your leaves resist withering.

Reflection Question: What root-deepening habit will help you trust God when conditions change?

Day 289

"The LORD is thy keeper... The sun shall not smite thee by day, nor the moon by night." — Psalm 121:5-6 (KJV)

As days shorten, nights stretch. God keeps you in both. He guards your going out and coming in, the bright hours and the midnight ones. Keeper is personal—think of a careful guardian watching the gate. He doesn't doze. You can sleep because He doesn't. When nighttime worries prowl, hand them to your Keeper and let rest be your yes.

Reflection Question: What nighttime fear will you hand to the Keeper so you can rest?

Day 290

"See then that ye walk circumspectly... Redeeming the time, because the days are evil." — Ephesians 5:15-16 (KJV)

Shorter daylight makes you notice time. Redeeming the time isn't cramming; it's being intentional. Walk circumspectly—eyes open, purpose clear. Say yes to what aligns with calling, no to what steals joy. A redeemed hour might be a neighbor chat, a focused project block, or a real Sabbath. Evil days won't set your agenda when wisdom walks you through.

Reflection Question: What small choice today would redeem an hour and make it meaningful?

Day 291

"Not forsaking the assembling of ourselves together... but exhorting one another:" — Hebrews 10:25a (KJV)

Fall groups restart. Community is not a bonus; it's a lifeline. Gathering doesn't have to be fancy—circle of chairs, shared snacks, open Bibles, honest talk. Exhorting sounds stiff, but it feels like, "Keep going," "I'm praying," "Here's truth." Isolation whispers lies; community sings truth louder. Show up imperfect. Bring your real self. God meets us in the together.

Reflection Question: Where can you commit to gather this month so encouragement has your name on it?

Day 292

"Wherefore comfort yourselves together, and edify one another," — 1 Thessalonians 5:11a (KJV)

Comfort and build—two hands of friendship. Comfort says, "I'm with you." Edify says, "Let's rise." Both matter. Texts after appointments, meals after loss, and also, "Have you considered...?" Building up isn't bossy; it's hopeful. We hold space for tears and for next steps. Your words can be lumber and blankets—shelter and structure.

Reflection Question: Who needs comfort or a gentle build-up from you before the week ends?

Day 293

"Honour the LORD with thy substance, and with the firstfruits of all thine increase:" — Proverbs 3:9 (KJV)

Budgets tighten heading toward holidays. Firstfruits remind us who provides. Honoring God first loosens the fear that money holds. It's not about amounts; it's about priority. Give before you spend, save with wisdom, live with open hands. Somehow generosity stretches what's left and sweetens your heart. God's been faithful; this honors that.

Reflection Question: What practical "first" can you give or set aside to honor God with your resources?

Day 294

"Come unto me, all ye that labour and are heavy laden, and I will give you rest." — Matthew 11:28 (KJV)

Some loads feel older than you—family patterns, work pressure, private worries. Jesus doesn't add advice first; He offers Himself. Rest here is a gift, not a reward. Coming looks like honesty: "I'm tired." His yoke fits; it doesn't chafe. Walking with Him won't erase the list, but it changes the weight. Trade your piled-up weariness for His paced-with-love way.

Reflection Question: Where can you come honestly to Jesus and let Him set a gentler pace?

Day 295

"Search me, O God, and know my heart... see if there be any wicked way in me, and lead me in the way everlasting." — Psalm 139:23-24 (KJV)

Autumn has us clearing closets; let God clear the heart. Invite His kind inspection—no dread, just truth. He reveals to heal. Maybe it's a quiet grudge, a hidden envy, a habit that keeps numbing. God doesn't shame; He leads—out of stuck places into steady paths. The everlasting way is solid ground under soft surrender.

Reflection Question: What might God be gently putting His finger on—and where could His leading take you instead?

Day 296

"He that hath knowledge spareth his words:" — Proverbs 17:27a (KJV)

Fall meetings stack up, and so do opinions. Wisdom often speaks less. Sparing words doesn't mean silence; it means choosing the few that heal or help. Count to three. Ask one more question. Let the room breathe before you fill it. Later, you'll be glad you edited in your head. Your restraint can lower the temperature and lift the tone.

Reflection Question: Where would fewer, wiser words do more good than many today?

Day 297

"Be sober, be vigilant; because your adversary the devil, as a roaring lion, walketh about," — 1 Peter 5:8a (KJV)

October brings costumes and pretend scares, but Scripture reminds us of a real enemy. Vigilant doesn't mean paranoid; it means awake. Notice patterns—fatigue that makes you snappy, old temptations knocking, fear disguising itself as "just being realistic." Sober-minded hearts ask for help fast and resist lies with truth. You're not defenseless; you're defended.

Reflection Question: What pattern needs your alertness and God's truth so the roar loses its power?

Day 298

"Rest in the LORD, and wait patiently for him:" — Psalm 37:7a (KJV)

Waiting feels like being stuck at a red light with no cars coming. Resting in God is putting the car in park and trusting the timing. Patience isn't passivity; it's quiet confidence that God is working while you're waiting. Trees don't rush their leaves to change; beauty comes right on time. Your season will turn when it should. Stay close. Breathe. Watch.

Reflection Question: Where can you practice restful waiting instead of restless worry this week?

Day 299

"All things work together for good to them that love God," — Romans 8:28a (KJV)

God is a master weaver. Threads you'd never choose—detours, losses, delays—get stitched into something strong and surprisingly beautiful. "Together" is the key word. On their own, some pieces hurt. In His hands, the pattern emerges. Loving God doesn't mean loving everything; it means trusting His artistry. One day you'll look back and see colors you missed up close.

Reflection Question: Which loose thread could you hand back to God, trusting He's weaving it into good?

Day 300

"For the LORD is good; his mercy is everlasting; and his truth endureth to all generations." — Psalm 100:5 (KJV)

Harvest time makes gratitude rise. God's goodness isn't seasonal; it's constant. Mercy doesn't expire at midnight. Truth doesn't update with trends. When news cycles churn, this verse steadies like a familiar song. Sing it to your heart, your kids, your fears. Generations change; God doesn't. That's worth a shout and a quiet smile.

Reflection Question: How will you celebrate God's unchanging goodness in one simple way today?

Day 301

"He which soweth bountifully shall reap also bountifully... for God loveth a cheerful giver." — *2 Corinthians 9:6-7 (KJV)*

Sowing in fall looks like generosity that trusts spring. Cheerful giving isn't forced; it's freed by remembering everything you have came from a generous God. Bountiful doesn't mean reckless; it means open-hearted—time, money, skills, attention. The joy is contagious. You get to be part of what God grows—in homes, churches, neighborhoods.

Reflection Question: What cheerful seed of generosity can you plant this week and trust God to grow?

Day 302

"Take therefore no thought for the morrow:" — *Matthew 6:34a (KJV)*

End-of-year pressure sneaks in—budgets, goals, holiday plans. Jesus invites you back to today. Tomorrow will have needs; you'll meet them with tomorrow's grace. "No thought" means don't be swallowed by worry. Do what you can, then let the rest sit in God's capable hands. Today has enough wonder and work to keep you here.

Reflection Question: What worry about tomorrow can you set down so you can be fully present today?

Day 303

"Put on therefore... bowels of mercies, kindness, humbleness of mind...
and above all these things put on charity," — Colossians 3:12, 14 (KJV)

October is layers season—sweater over shirt, scarf over sweater. Paul says dress your soul the same way: mercy, kindness, humility, patience—and love on top like a warm coat. You won't always feel these, but you can choose to wear them. People will feel the warmth. Love is the layer that ties the outfit together.

Reflection Question: Which "layer" do you need to put on first so love can sit on top today?

Day 304

"Behold, I stand at the door, and knock:" — Revelation 3:20a (KJV)

Doorbells ring more in fall—neighbors, deliveries, friends. Jesus knocks too. Not kicking down, just knocking. He wants to come in—not to inspect, but to share a meal, steady the room, bring peace. Sometimes the door is crowded with hurry, shame, or distraction. Clear the entry. Open up. A simple, "Come in, Lord," can turn an average evening holy.

Reflection Question: What might it look like for you to open the door to Jesus in the middle of your ordinary today?

November: Gratitude in Motion

Day 305

"O give thanks unto the LORD, for he is good: for his mercy endureth for ever." — Psalm 107:1 (KJV)

November leans us toward gratitude—leaf piles, warm soups, early sunsets. This verse gives the why behind our thanks: God is good, and His mercy doesn't run out. Not when the budget squeezes. Not when the day disappoints. Think of a bottomless coffee pot that never burns—fresh mercy, poured again. Gratitude isn't ignoring pain; it's noticing grace in the middle of it. A quick "thank You" for a quiet commute, a friend's text, or a moment of peace can reset your mood. You don't have to feel grateful to start; starting often stirs the feeling. Let your thanks be small and sincere. God hears every "thank You" like a child's laugh—gladly and often.

Reflection Question: What simple mercy can you notice and thank God for before the day moves on?

Day 306

"In every thing give thanks: for this is the will of God in Christ Jesus concerning you." — 1 Thessalonians 5:18 (KJV)

We ask about God's will; Paul gives one clear piece—give thanks in everything. Not for everything, but in it. The meeting that shifted. The meal that burned. The plan that delayed. Gratitude invites God into the middle and changes your posture from clenched to open. It can be as small as "Thank You for help coming," or "Thank You I'm not alone." Think of adding light to a dim room; it doesn't change the furniture, but you see differently. This practice keeps you from waiting on perfect circumstances to live a joyful life. Thanks in the mess is brave faith in real time.

Reflection Question: Where can you speak a quiet "thank You" right in the middle of something unfinished?

Day 307

"And let the peace of God rule in your hearts... and be ye thankful." — Colossians 3:15 (KJV)

Holidays can crowd the calendar and the heart. Paul pairs peace and thankfulness like gloves that fit together. Let peace "rule"—call the shots—when stress tries to take over. Thankfulness helps that happen. When you choose to notice what's right before listing what's wrong, peace gets a vote. Picture an umpire making a close call; gratitude often tips the play toward calm. You don't manufacture peace; you make room for it by remembering God's steady care. A thankful sentence in a tense moment is surprisingly strong medicine.

Reflection Question: What moment today could shift if you let peace rule by choosing gratitude first?

Day 308

"The LORD is my shepherd; I shall not want." — Psalm 23:1 (KJV)

"Shepherd" is personal. Not a manager, a guide. He leads, feeds, watches, rescues. When your list grows and energy shrinks, remember who's tending you. "I shall not want" doesn't mean you'll get everything; it means you won't lack what your soul truly needs: guidance, comfort, courage, rest. Think of a hand on a sheep's back, steadying it through narrow places. Your Shepherd knows the path through November's rush. Slow down enough to walk with Him—one step, one task, one conversation at a time.

Reflection Question: Where do you need to stop hustling and follow your Shepherd's steady pace?

Day 309

"I have learned, in whatsoever state I am, therewith to be content." — Philippians 4:11b (KJV)

Contentment doesn't show up on sale; it's learned. Paul practiced it in plenty and in shortage. It's not settling for less; it's trusting God with the now while aiming for the next. That looks like blessing the apartment you have while saving for a house, enjoying a simple dinner when you imagined something fancier, or smiling at a small win. Contentment even quiets comparison at the big table—it frees you to cheer others without shrinking yourself. It's a skill you can practice, not a mood you wait for.

Reflection Question: What can you genuinely bless about your current season while you keep moving forward?

Day 310

"So teach us to number our days, that we may apply our hearts unto wisdom." — Psalm 90:12 (KJV)

Shorter daylight makes time feel precious. Numbering your days isn't morbid; it's mindful. When you remember time is finite, you spend it better—fewer autopilot scrolls, more face-to-face moments; less "someday," more "today." Wisdom flows from attention: What matters? Who matters? You won't fit everything in—but you can fit in the right things. Imagine a basket at the end of the day; what do you want to find inside?

Reflection Question: What small adjustment could help you spend today like it actually matters?

Day 311

"But they that wait upon the LORD shall renew their strength; they shall mount up with wings as eagles;" — Isaiah 40:31a (KJV)

Waiting sounds like doing nothing, but with God it's a trade—your strain for His strength. Renewal happens when you stop flapping and catch His wind. Think of an eagle using currents you can't see, rising without panic. Waiting might look like praying before replying, resting before deciding, or not forcing a door. You don't miss out by waiting on God; you're fitted to fly when the time is right.

Reflection Question: Where do you need to pause and let God's strength lift you instead of your effort?

Day 312

"But to do good and to communicate forget not: for with such sacrifices God is well pleased." — Hebrews 13:16 (KJV)

As the giving season starts, Scripture keeps it simple: do good and share. Communicate here means "share what you have"—time, money, rides, skills, a table. It may feel like a sacrifice when life is full. God notices and smiles. You don't need a campaign; you need a yes. Small generosity often lands as big love.

Reflection Question: What can you share this week—a ride, a meal, a skill—that would quietly bless someone?

Day 313

"Better is a dry morsel, and quietness therewith, than an house full of sacrifices with strife." — Proverbs 17:1 (KJV)

Holiday meals can carry high expectations. This proverb says peace beats a perfect spread. A simple table with calm conversation is richer than a fancy one with tension. Quietness doesn't mean no laughter; it means hearts at rest. Maybe that looks like lowering the bar on the menu, setting a kind tone, or steering away from known hot topics. People remember how they felt more than what they ate.

Reflection Question: What can you do to help your table be peaceful, even if everything isn't perfect?

Day 314

"Every good gift and every perfect gift is from above, and cometh down from the Father of lights," — James 1:17a (KJV)

Trace the arrows back. The friend who checked in. The heater that works. The conversation that healed. Good gifts aren't random; they come down with love. Naming them turns ordinary days into altars. It also keeps you from grabbing credit too tightly—gratitude opens your hands to receive and to give. The "Father of lights" doesn't flicker; He's steady. So are His gifts, even when they arrive in plain wrapping.

Reflection Question: Which everyday gift will you trace back to God and thank Him for out loud today?

Day 315

"I will bless the LORD at all times: his praise shall continually be in my mouth." — Psalm 34:1 (KJV)

"All times" includes a rough Wednesday and a sweet Sunday. Continual praise is a choice to keep God's goodness in your mouth even when life tastes bitter. Try sprinkling praise like salt across your day—on the commute, in the line, after the email. Blessing God doesn't shrink hard things; it enlarges your view of Him. And that changes how you carry what's heavy.

Reflection Question: Where can a quick sentence of praise interrupt a complaint that's been looping?

Day 316

"Martha, Martha, thou art careful and troubled about many things:
But one thing is needful." — Luke 10:41-42a (KJV)

Busy is loud in November—lists, guests, deadlines. Jesus doesn't scold Martha's service; He invites her back to the one necessary thing—Him. Sitting with Jesus first doesn't cancel serving; it cleanses it from hurry and resentment. Think of letting the sink fill while you sit with your coffee and Scripture. Ten minutes can shift the whole house's tone. Choose presence before performance whenever you can.

Reflection Question: What "one thing" with Jesus will you protect so everything else flows better?

Day 317

"It is of the LORD'S mercies that we are not consumed... They are new
every morning: great is thy faithfulness." — Lamentations 3:22-23
(KJV)

Some years drain you more than others. This promise meets you at daybreak: new mercy. Not leftovers. Fresh. You might wake up to the same challenges, but you don't wake up to the same supply. God refills. Faithfulness means He won't forget you in the swirl of the season. Collect small proofs—strength for a hard call, a laugh you needed, the right words at the right time. That's mercy on your doorstep.

Reflection Question: Where did you see a fresh mercy recently—and how does it change today's outlook?

Day 318

"Being enriched in every thing to all bountifulness, which causeth through us thanksgiving to God." — 2 Corinthians 9:11 (KJV)

God enriches you so generosity can flow through you. Bountifulness isn't about wealth; it's about readiness to give—encouragement, help, money, time. Your giving sparks thanksgiving to God in other hearts. It's a circle of grace. When you feel stretched, remember: you're a river, not a reservoir. Trust God to keep you supplied as you pour.

Reflection Question: How could your generosity this week lead someone else to thank God?

Day 319

"They that sow in tears shall reap in joy." — Psalm 126:5 (KJV)

Some seeds are planted with wet cheeks—prayers for a prodigal, quiet endurance at work, forgiveness that costs you. Sowing in tears isn't failure; it's faith under pressure. Joy may not come overnight, but God promises harvest. Look for early shoots—small changes, open doors, softer hearts. Keep planting the right things even when it stings. Joy grows in fields watered by trust.

Reflection Question: What tearful sowing will you keep at, believing God for a joyful harvest?

Day 320

"The liberal soul shall be made fat: and he that watereth shall be watered also himself." — Proverbs 11:25 (KJV)

Generous people rarely run dry. Somehow, as you pour, God refills. "Made fat" means well-nourished—soul and sometimes even supply. Watering others can be a note, a babysit, a coffee, a gift. You don't give to get; you give because love is your family trait now. Watch how your own life feels fuller when you help someone else bloom.

Reflection Question: Who could you "water" this week—practically or personally—so both of you are refreshed?

Day 321

"What shall I render unto the LORD for all his benefits toward me? I will take the cup of salvation, and call upon the name of the LORD." — Psalm 116:12-13 (KJV)

What do you give the God who has everything? You receive what He offers. That's the surprise of gratitude in Scripture—return thanks by taking the cup He hands: salvation, help, fellowship. Calling on His name honors Him more than impressing Him. It's like a child saying thank you by climbing into your lap. God loves when you enjoy what He gives.

Reflection Question: How will you "take the cup" today—receiving grace and calling on God with a thankful heart?

Day 322

"All the days of the afflicted are evil: but he that is of a merry heart hath a continual feast." — Proverbs 15:15 (KJV)

A merry heart doesn't ignore reality; it looks for joy within it. A "continual feast" sounds like Thanksgiving spread vibes—laughter, stories, warmth. You can taste that on a random Tuesday: a song you love, a sunset that refuses to be normal, a joke in the kitchen. Joy isn't a luxury; it's soul nutrition. Choose small celebrations and watch your appetite for hope return.

Reflection Question: What tiny "feast" can you enjoy today to feed a merry heart?

Day 323

"For where your treasure is, there will your heart be also." — Matthew 6:21 (KJV)

Budgets bump into values this time of year. Jesus connects money and heart, not to shame you but to free you. Treasure follows love. Invest in what truly matters—people, purpose, kindness, integrity. It might shift how you spend, save, and give. Think beyond price tags: your attention is treasure too. Where you place it, your heart settles.

Reflection Question: How could your spending—or your attention—better reflect what you truly value this month?

Day 324

"Use hospitality one to another without grudging." — 1 Peter 4:9 (KJV)

Hospitality is more about presence than performance. People want a place to exhale, not perfect centerpieces. Without grudging means open-hearted, not eye-twitching at the crumbs. Paper plates are allowed. Soup counts. Your welcome may be the softest place someone visits all week. And in opening your door, you might find your own heart warmed.

Reflection Question: What simple, low-stress way could you offer real welcome to someone soon?

Day 325

"Trust in the LORD, and do good; so shalt thou dwell in the land, and verily thou shalt be fed." — Psalm 37:3 (KJV)

Trust pairs with action. Do the next good thing while you rely on God for the bigger picture. "Dwell" suggests planting, not pacing. "Fed" hints at provision coming as you stay faithful. That could mean applying for the job and leaving the outcome, making the meal and letting God soften the conversation, or finishing the task and trusting Him with favor.

Reflection Question: What next good step will you take today as an act of trust in God's care?

Day 326

"Wherefore we receiving a kingdom which cannot be moved, let us have grace, whereby we may serve God acceptably..." — Hebrews 12:28 (KJV)

Everything on your calendar moves—events, meetings, even plans—but God's kingdom does not. That stability shifts how you serve. Grace becomes your fuel, not pressure. Serving acceptably looks like worship in motion—heart engaged, ego quiet. When you remember you belong to an unshakable kingdom, you serve with calm courage, even when schedules wobble.

Reflection Question: How does remembering an unshakable kingdom change the way you serve this week?

Day 327

"Thou art good, and doest good; teach me thy statutes." — Psalm 119:68 (KJV)

God's goodness isn't mood-based; it's who He is. He does good, even when we can't see all the angles. That reality makes His commands feel like guidance, not grit-your-teeth rules. "Teach me" is a learner's heart—open to correction and direction. Let His goodness frame the way you listen and obey. It's easier to trust instructions from Someone who's always kind.

Reflection Question: What instruction from God would be easier to follow if you started with "You are good"?

Day 328

"Therewith bless we God... and therewith curse we men... My brethren, these things ought not so to be." — James 3:9-10 (KJV)

Same mouth, two directions. It's jarring to sing on Sunday and slice with sarcasm on Monday. James says, "This doesn't fit." Blessing people who bear God's image lines up your words with your worship. That may look like pausing before a snarky reply, changing the subject, or finding a true good to name. Your tongue can turn a table into a sanctuary or a storm. Choose the sanctuary.

Reflection Question: Where can you switch from sharp to blessing so your words match your worship?

Day 329

"Rejoice with them that do rejoice, and weep with them that weep." — Romans 12:15 (KJV)

Holidays hold both—celebration and ache. Love shows up tuned to the moment. When your friend gets good news, throw confetti with her. When another faces an empty chair, sit quietly and pass the tissues. You don't have to fix; you just have to be with. Shared joy doubles; shared sorrow halves. This is community at its most human and holy.

Reflection Question: Who around you needs your laughter—or your tears—this week?

Day 330

"Surely I have behaved and quieted myself, as a child that is weaned of his mother:" — Psalm 131:2 (KJV)

This picture is tender—contentment without clutching. A weaned child rests near Mom, not for milk but for nearness. That's mature trust. Instead of demanding specific outcomes, you settle into God's presence. It's not passivity; it's peace. Try a few minutes of quiet—hands open, shoulders down, whisper, "I'm with You." Let love steady you more than answers satisfy you.

Reflection Question: How could you practice a few minutes of quieted trust and let God's nearness be enough?

Day 331

"Give thanks unto the LORD, call upon his name, make known his deeds among the people." — 1 Chronicles 16:8 (KJV)

Thanks naturally spills into testimony. Call on His name, then tell what happened—simple, unpolished, true. "We prayed, and the test came back clear." "I was anxious, but His peace held me." Stories spread courage like warm bread at the table—everyone eats better. You don't need a platform; you need a conversation.

Reflection Question: What small story of God's goodness can you share with someone this week?

Day 332

"Forbearing one another, and forgiving one another... even as Christ forgave you, so also do ye." — Colossians 3:13 (KJV)

Family and friends gather—and so do quirks. Forbearance is patience with real people in real time. Forgiveness releases debts so connection can breathe. Christ's forgiveness becomes your reference point—lavish, undeserved, freeing. Remembering that softens your stance and loosens your grip on petty hurts. It also gives courage to address real wrongs with grace.

Reflection Question: Where could patience or forgiveness make the room lighter during this season?

Day 333

"Let nothing be done through strife or vainglory; but in lowliness of mind let each esteem other better than themselves... Look not every man on his own things, but every man also on the things of others." — Philippians 2:3-4 (KJV)

Holiday pressure can make us self-protective. Paul invites another way: humble attention. Esteeming others means choosing their good without losing yourself—listening fully, letting someone else shine, taking the smaller slice. This isn't erasing you; it's freeing you from the need to win the room. Joy sneaks in when we make space for each other.

Reflection Question: What practical way can you put someone else first and enjoy the freedom of it?

Day 334

"For the kingdom of God is not meat and drink; but righteousness, and peace, and joy in the Holy Ghost." — Romans 14:17 (KJV)

November centers on meals, but God's kingdom centers on more—right relationships, deep peace, Spirit-given joy. Food matters; fellowship matters more. Don't let menu stress steal kingdom gifts. Aim for rooms where people feel safe, seen, and glad to be together. When righteousness and peace sit at your table, joy usually pulls up a chair.

Reflection Question: How can you prioritize righteousness, peace, and Spirit-joy over menu perfection this month?

December: God With Us

Day 335

"For unto us a child is born, unto us a son is given... and his name shall be called Wonderful, Counsellor, The mighty God," — Isaiah 9:6 (KJV)

Christmas begins with a gift, not a demand. A Child arrives carrying titles bigger than any stocking: Wonderful, Counsellor, Mighty God. That's more than a nativity scene—it's help for your actual life. Need wisdom for a hard talk? Counsellor. Feel small against big problems? Mighty God. Wonder feels thin this late in the year, after emails and errands. But wonder grows when you slow and look again: God came close as a baby. Fragile on purpose. Near on purpose. He entered noise and need so yours wouldn't scare Him off. Let the names rest on you like a warm coat. Try whispering the one you need most today and see how your shoulders drop.

Reflection Question: Which name—Wonderful, Counsellor, Mighty God—do you most need to lean on right now?

Day 336

"Behold, I bring you good tidings of great joy... For unto you is born this day a Saviour," — Luke 2:10-11 (KJV)

Good news still breaks into ordinary nights. Shepherds were working the late shift, probably cold and bored, when heaven lit up. The angel didn't announce a new rule; he announced joy. Not generic—"unto you." This is personal joy that meets you in traffic, on a couch with wrapping paper everywhere, in a hospital room. A Saviour is born, and that means rescue where you can't rescue yourself. Great joy doesn't always feel loud. Sometimes it's a deep steadiness under the bustle—"I am loved. I am not alone. Help has come."

Reflection Question: Where could you receive "unto you" joy today—in the middle of your ordinary?

Day 337

"They shall call his name Emmanuel, which being interpreted is, God with us." — Matthew 1:23 (KJV)

With us. Not above us, against us, or just watching us—God moved in. Think of a friend who sits on the kitchen floor with you when life unravels. That's the feel of Emmanuel. December holds loud rooms and quiet aches. "With us" covers both. When crowds overwhelm, He's near. When the evening feels empty, He's near. You don't have to climb up to Him; He came down to you. If your prayers feel thin, try plain words: "Jesus, be with me here." Emmanuel turns any space into holy ground—car, break room, grocery aisle.

Reflection Question: What part of your day needs you to breathe, "God is with me here," and live like it's true?

Day 338

"And the Word was made flesh, and dwelt among us," — John 1:14 (KJV)

God put on skin. He didn't send a memo; He moved into the neighborhood. He learned a trade, took long walks, laughed at parties, cried at graves. If you've ever wondered whether God understands real life—He does. Dwelling among us means He's comfortable in kitchens and cubicles, in car lines and waiting rooms. Your faith doesn't have to be lofty to be real; it can look like inviting Jesus into a grocery list and a grief. Sacred isn't far away; it's here because He is.

Reflection Question: Where could you let Jesus "dwell" with you today—in something as ordinary as dinner or errands?

Day 339

"When the fulness of the time was come, God sent forth his Son," — Galatians 4:4 (KJV)

God's timing is rarely our timing, but it's always right. "Fullness" sounds like a cup finally filled to the brim. History, roads, language—everything lined up for Jesus' arrival. Your story has a fullness moment too. Delays aren't denial; sometimes they're careful setup. Think of bread rising under a towel—it looks like nothing for a while, then it's ready. You don't have to force what God is fitting. Keep being faithful. The sending comes when it should.

Reflection Question: What are you waiting on that might need "fullness" rather than force—and how can you rest there?

Day 340

"But thou, Bethlehem... out of thee shall he come forth unto me that is to be ruler in Israel;" — Micah 5:2 (KJV)

Small town, big story. Bethlehem wasn't the obvious choice, but God loves unlikely places. That's good news for ordinary apartments, simple kitchens, and quiet offices. Great things start small—prayers whispered half-awake, a text that begins a reconciliation, a budget that makes room to bless. Don't despise your "Bethlehem." God writes headlines in humble spaces.

Reflection Question: What small, unnoticed place in your life might be where God wants to begin something beautiful?

Day 341

"Behold the handmaid of the Lord; be it unto me according to thy word." — Luke 1:38 (KJV)

Mary said yes without a full plan. That takes trust. Your December might hold invitations that stretch you—hosting when you feel shy, giving when funds feel tight, stepping back when you usually fix. A surrendered "be it unto me" isn't passive; it's brave agreement with God's good heart. You don't have to see every step to take the first one. God's word holds you better than a detailed itinerary.

Reflection Question: Where could a simple "yes, Lord" be your next step—even without all the answers?

Day 342

"Joseph... fear not to take unto thee Mary thy wife:" — Matthew 1:20 (KJV)

Joseph's obedience was quiet and costly. No speech, no spotlight—just a steady yes in a complicated story. Advent honors that kind of faith. Maybe your role this month is steady: covering a shift, shouldering logistics, choosing trust over image. Fear not to take what God places in your care, even if others don't get it. Heaven notices the hidden yes.

Reflection Question: What faithful, quiet obedience is in front of you—and how can you take it without fear?

Day 343

"But Mary kept all these things, and pondered them in her heart." — Luke 2:19 (KJV)

Pondering is a lost art in a push-notification season. Mary didn't post; she kept and considered. Make a little room for holy noticing—write down a mercy, sit with a verse, replay a conversation where God felt near. Pondering turns moments into meaning. It slows the season down enough for your soul to catch up.

Reflection Question: What could you "keep and ponder" today so it doesn't blur into everything else?

Day 344

"Glory to God in the highest, and on earth peace, good will toward men." — Luke 2:14 (KJV)

Angels sang peace, not perfection. Peace doesn't mean every plan lands; it means hearts lean toward goodwill. December family rooms need that. So do group chats and checkout lines. Peace starts small—tone, timing, assuming the best. Glory up, peace out. When God is big in your eyes, pettiness shrinks. You become a calm place in a crowded month.

Reflection Question: Where can you offer goodwill today so peace has room to grow?

Day 345

"Now the God of hope fill you with all joy and peace in believing," — Romans 15:13 (KJV)

Hope is not wishful thinking; it's a Person pouring joy and peace as you trust Him. Believing is the funnel—open it, and He fills. This can look like handing Him one worry at a time and watching the weight shift. Joy and peace don't always roar; sometimes they hum under the noise, keeping you from fraying. Ask to be filled. Then notice the quiet steadiness that follows.

Reflection Question: What would it look like to open your "funnel" of trust and let God fill you with hope today?

Day 346

"And the light shineth in darkness; and the darkness comprehended it not." — John 1:5 (KJV)

Candles glow brighter in December because nights are long. Jesus' light doesn't argue with darkness; it simply shines, and darkness can't swallow it. If sadness or stress shadows your month, you're not defective—you're human. Bring the dark to the Light. Read a Gospel, pray a psalm, invite a friend in. Light isn't fragile, and you don't have to fake bright. Let His steady glow be enough while you heal and hope.

Reflection Question: Where do you need to stop wrestling the dark and simply sit in Jesus' light?

Day 347

"Though he was rich, yet for your sakes he became poor," — 2 Corinthians 8:9 (KJV)

Christmas generosity starts with Jesus. He traded heaven's richness for a manger's straw and a carpenter's wage—so we could become rich in grace. Giving then becomes a response, not a performance. It might be money, yes, but also time, attention, and patience. Give from what He gave you: comfort to the hurting, presence to the lonely, forgiveness where it's overdue. That's luxury in God's economy.

Reflection Question: What kind of "rich" from Jesus could you pass along to someone this week?

Day 348

"After that the kindness and love of God our Saviour toward man appeared... not by works of righteousness which we have done, but according to his mercy he saved us," — Titus 3:4-5 (KJV)

Advent is God's kindness showing up with skin on. Salvation isn't a merit badge; it's mercy. That takes the pressure off December. You don't earn God's smile by nailing the season. You receive it and then reflect it. Let kindness be your theme—extra patience in lines, heartfelt thanks to workers, a slower tone at home. Mercy showed up for you; let it show through you.

Reflection Question: Where can you swap performance for receiving mercy—and then pass that mercy on?

Day 349

"The dayspring from on high hath visited us, To give light to them that sit in darkness," — Luke 1:78-79 (KJV)

Dayspring is dawn talk—light easing over the horizon, not blinding, just faithful. God visits the places that feel stuck in night: grief, uncertainty, regret. He doesn't shout at the shadows; He turns on morning. Sometimes you don't need a miracle; you need a sunrise. Watch for it in a verse that lands, a friend who calls, a calmer heart than yesterday. That's dayspring visiting.

Reflection Question: What "sunrise" sign of God's nearness can you watch for as this day unfolds?

Day 350

"When they saw the star, they rejoiced with exceeding great joy." —
Matthew 2:10 (KJV)

The wise men followed a light step by step, not knowing the whole route. Guidance often looks like that. You get a nudge, a clue, a door. Walk toward it. Joy grows as you move, not as you map everything. When they arrived, their joy spilled into worship and gifts. That's a good rhythm: notice God's guidance, rejoice, and respond with what you have.

Reflection Question: What "star" are you seeing—a small guidance—and how can you step toward it with joy?

Day 351

"Peace I leave with you, my peace I give unto you." — *John 14:27 (KJV)*

Jesus doesn't loan peace; He leaves it like a will. "My peace"— the kind that slept in storms and loved under pressure. You can't buy this peace with candles or playlists, though those help. You receive it, again and again, by trusting the Giver. When anxiety shouts, try a breath prayer: "Your peace, Jesus." Then take the next unhurried step. Peace is not the absence of noise; it's the presence of Christ.

Reflection Question: Where do you need to receive—not manufacture—Jesus' peace today?

Day 352

"He made himself of no reputation... and became obedient unto death,"
— Philippians 2:7-8 (KJV)

Christmas crowds love reputation—who hosted best, dressed best, posted best. Jesus chose the opposite: no reputation, servant form. Humility isn't self-hate; it's self-forgetful love. It looks like letting someone else be first, doing what needs doing without credit, apologizing quickly. Ironically, that's where joy sneaks in. When the room stops being about you, you can actually enjoy the room.

Reflection Question: What would no-reputation love look like in one practical choice today?

Day 353

"In this was manifested the love of God toward us, because that God sent his only begotten Son into the world," — 1 John 4:9 (KJV)

Love isn't abstract; it's embodied. God sent, we receive. If you've wondered how God feels about you, look at Christmas—love moved toward you. Let that soften the inner critic and quiet the hustle to be enough. Then mirror it: move toward someone with love that fits—listening, a note, a warm bowl, a ride. Love shows up.

Reflection Question: Who could you move toward with God-shaped love before the day ends?

Day 354

"Thanks be unto God for his unspeakable gift." — *2 Corinthians 9:15 (KJV)*

Some gifts are hard to describe—laughter that heals, timing that feels uncanny, a Savior who brings us home. "Unspeakable" doesn't mean silent; it means too rich for full words. Still, try. Thank God specifically: for Jesus, for rescue, for the way He keeps finding you. Gratitude turns December from pressure into praise. You start seeing gifts under every tree—mercy here, help there, hope everywhere.

Reflection Question: What words of thanks—imperfect but real—will you offer for God's "unspeakable" gift?

Day 355

"Inasmuch as ye have done it unto one of the least of these... ye have done it unto me." — *Matthew 25:40 (KJV)*

Jesus hides in plain sight—in the neighbor, the cashier, the relative who's hard to love. Serving them is serving Him. That changes errands and gatherings. A patient tone becomes worship. A tip becomes joy. A ride to the appointment becomes an offering. You won't meet a person today who isn't loved by God. Let that truth set your pace and your face.

Reflection Question: Who is your "least of these" today, and how can you love Jesus by loving them?

Day 356

"The LORD is nigh unto them that are of a broken heart;" — *Psalm 34:18 (KJV)*

Not everyone feels merry, and that's okay. God draws near to the brokenhearted. He doesn't rush you past grief; He sits with you in it. If this December holds an empty chair, a diagnosis, or a dream delayed, you're not failing Christmas. You're being held. Let friends help. Let tears come. Let Jesus be enough company for a quiet night. Nearness is His gift to the hurting.

Reflection Question: Where do you need to let God's nearness meet you in a place that aches?

Day 357

"Comfort ye, comfort ye my people, saith your God." — *Isaiah 40:1 (KJV)*

Comfort is God's assignment to His people, not just a Hallmark mood. Comfort looks like presence, blankets, soup, silence, true words. It's not fixing; it's with-ness. You can be a soft place for someone to land this month. Ask God who needs comfort through you—then keep it simple and steady. Your calm can be a bridge back to hope.

Reflection Question: Who could use God's comfort through you—and what gentle step can you take?

Day 358

"Let the heavens rejoice, and let the earth be glad;" — *Psalm 96:11 (KJV)*

Creation throws its own carols—frost sparkling, stars sharp, air crisp. Joy is appropriate. Celebration is spiritual. Let yourself laugh loud, sing off-key, bake the recipe that makes memories. Rejoicing doesn't cancel sorrow; it tells a bigger story: God is worthy. In a year that held both bruises and blessings, choose a pocket of gladness and fill it.

Reflection Question: What little celebration—song, walk, treat—will you enjoy as an act of worship?

Day 359

"For mine eyes have seen thy salvation," — *Luke 2:30 (KJV)*

Simeon waited long and then held the Answer in his arms. Some prayers take years; then a moment arrives and you whisper, "I see it." Salvation is bigger than a fix; it's a Person who keeps showing up. Look back over your year—where did you glimpse God's saving work? A softened heart, a settled fear, a steady provision? Name it. Holding those moments builds faith for the ones still in process.

Reflection Question: Where have your eyes seen God's saving work this year, even in small ways?

Day 360

"By him all things consist." — Colossians 1:17b (KJV)

When the calendar feels like Jenga, remember who holds the tower. Jesus sustains everything—galaxies and grocery lists. If your December is wobbling, ask Him to hold what you can't: relationships, finances, timelines. Consist means hold together. You don't have to be the glue; you know the One who is. Do the next faithful thing. Let Him keep the pieces from scattering.

Reflection Question: What will you place back into Jesus' hands today so He can hold it together?

Day 361

"Behold, I will do a new thing; now it shall spring forth;" — Isaiah 43:19a (KJV)

As the year winds down, God speaks future. New thing doesn't always mean big thing—it can be a fresh habit, a healed relationship, a brave yes. New often springs, not stumbles; it surprises with life. You don't have to drum it up; you make room. Clear a little space—time, headroom, heartroom—and watch for green shoots. God loves beginnings.

Reflection Question: What small space can you clear so God's "new thing" has room to spring up?

Day 362

"Thou crownest the year with thy goodness;" — Psalm 65:11a (KJV)

Crown is a finishing word—God sets goodness like a wreath on the year. Not because every moment was easy, but because His kindness ran through it. Gather your snapshots: answered texts, protected trips, lessons learned, unexpected laughter. Name them out loud or write them down. Crowning the year with gratitude helps you carry hope into the next one.

Reflection Question: What three evidences of God's goodness will you place like a crown on this year?

Day 363

"Jesus Christ the same yesterday, and to day, and for ever." — Hebrews 13:8 (KJV)

Trends shift, plans pivot, kids outgrow shoes. Jesus doesn't change. The One in the manger is the Lord of your Monday. The same compassion, the same strength, the same truth. That steadiness lets you be flexible without falling apart. As you glance back and look ahead, anchor to the Unchanging. New year, same Savior—that's enough.

Reflection Question: How does Jesus' unchanging nature steady a worry about the year ahead?

Day 364

"Behold, I make all things new." — Revelation 21:5a (KJV)

This is God's long promise—new everything. No more tears, no more decay. We taste it in small ways now: restored friendships, forgiven sins, fresh starts. One day it will be complete. Let that future hope leak into your present—clean a corner, apologize first, try again. Newness isn't naive; it's faith in the One who writes the last chapter.

Reflection Question: Where can you practice a small "new" today as a nod to God's big New?

Day 365

"The LORD bless thee, and keep thee: The LORD make his face shine upon thee... and give thee peace." — Numbers 6:24-26 (KJV)

Endings and beginnings need blessing. God's face toward you—warm, attentive—changes everything. Kept means guarded when you don't even know what to guard against. Peace is His parting gift and your starting place. Receive this like hands open for a present. Let it rest on your home, your work, your body, your dreams. Step into the new year under a smile that won't fade.

Reflection Question: How will you receive this blessing—personally and specifically—as you step into what's next?

OUR BOOKS

Start each day with purpose, peace, and spiritual renewal.

Whether you're walking solo, side by side with a partner, or seeking strength for the journey ahead—this devotional series meets you right where you are.

Collect the Whole Series

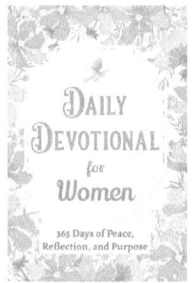 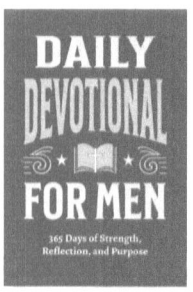 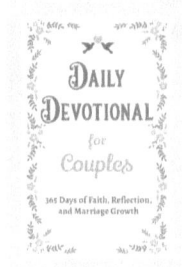

Daily Devotional for Women

Daily Devotional for Men

Daily Devotional for Couples

Available at:

• Amazon

• Barnes & Noble

• Major online bookstores

Each book is a spiritual companion. Together, they form a complete journey—personal, relational, and transformative.

Don't wait—bring home the full devotional set and let every day draw you closer to faith, love, and lasting renewal.